To the Ralphs

Edward J. Rohn

WHILE THE EAGLE SLEEPS

Edward J. Robinson

Published by World Audience, Inc.
(www.worldaudience.org)
303 Park Avenue South, Suite 1440
New York, NY 10010-3657
Phone (646) 620-7406; Fax (646) 620-7406
info@worldaudience.org
ISBN 978-1-935444-75-6

DEDICATION

This work is dedicated to my eight grandchildren: Jason Pustulka, Kaitlin, Ryan, Clare, Molly and Jack Robinson, and Ben and Betsy Robinson. I pray that the United States into which you grow up becomes the shining star that it once was, and that I imagine it can be again.

You must do your part.

TABLE OF CONTENTS

INTRODUCTION

In 1938, Winston Churchill wrote *While England Slept*, highlighting England's lack of preparation for the threat of Nazi Germany. In 1940, John F. Kennedy, while a senior at Harvard University, responded to Churchill's book by writing *Why England Slept*. Kennedy wrote in his introduction, "This book is an attempt to explain why England slept. I have started with the assumption that there is no shortcut answer to this problem. To me it appears extremely shortsighted to dismiss, superficially, England's present position as a result of one man's or one group of men's blindness."

Kennedy continued, "Given the conditions of a Democratic government, a free press, public elections, and a cabinet responsible to the Parliament and thus to the people, given rule by the majority, it is unreasonable to blame the entire situation on one man or one group."

Unlike England in 1938 or 1940, the United States today is not just on the brink of war; the United States is now in a war, and we are losing. I am not talking about Iraq or Afghanistan. The war I am referring to is an economic war. This war began slowly and quietly in the late 1970s and has continued unabated until today, with the assistance of several presidential administrations and Congresses, both Democrat and Republican. This economic war, spurred by mergers, free trade, and loss of individual purchasing power has caused the U.S. to fight for its life as the world's economic power. As a consequence, the U.S. is also fighting for its political and military leadership.

This economic tsunami began under President Carter, but really picked up steam during the Reagan terms, and then spread and expanded under the Clinton and the G.W. Bush administrations.

Our enemies are akin to the Four Horsemen of the Apocalypse. The Four Horsemen mentioned in the Book of Revelation and in Greek mythology are Pestilence, War (Destruction), Famine and Death. In 1924, Grantland Rice, a famous sports writer for the New York Tribune, revisited the Four Horsemen. Writing about the Notre Dame football team that beat Army, Rice started his story about the game: "Outlined against a blue-gray October sky, the Four Horsemen rode again. In dramatic lore, they are known as famine, pestilence, destruction and death. These are only aliases. Their real names are Stuhldreher, Miller, Crowley and Layden."

Rice wrote about football. Today's versions of the Four Horsemen are Corporations Without Borders, Moneyism, The Broken Health Industry and Government for Half the People.

In *Why England Slept*, Kennedy quoted Prime Minister Stanley Baldwin's 1938 address to Parliament. Baldwin stated that democratic governments are at least two years behind a totalitarian nation regarding manufacturing. This was true in armaments, when a willing nation could crank up its production to close the gap in two years. In economics, however, in a nation that has been propagandized to believe that unrestricted free trade, with totally unrestricted commerce, is good for every U.S. citizen, the gap created by this facade can never be closed in a two-year span. We may never again be the strongest economic or military power in the world.

The graveyard of fallen economic nations is marked with the tombstones of Persia, Rome, Greece, Egypt, Spain, Portugal, France and Great Britain. Some countries that were beaten militarily subsequently rose to economic power, such as Japan, China and Germany. But many other nations, while overcoming the physical defeats of war, could not overcome the economic blows incurred, and never regained their strength.

The question remains: Is there a parallel between the post-World War I depression era and our current situation in the U.S.? Since the initiation of Social Security, unemployment insurance and welfare, it is unlikely that we will suffer through another Great Depression. However, unless we act, we will suffer in many other ways.

When a nation's economy is not based on the production of goods or services, that nation will fail as a major economic power. Wall Street has become a betting house in which investors gamble on stock prices going up or down. It holds people's money in the form of betting slips that have no intrinsic value. When the price of a particular share exceeds the real value per share of the company, Wall Street becomes a trading house where shares are traded back and forth without attribution to real value.

Every presidential administration since President Carter's, whether Republican or Democrat, has virtually ignored many of our regulatory laws and the criminal consequences. Uncontrolled free enterprise has caused merger mania, and the U.S. Attorney General's Mergers and Acquisitions

Division has been inundated with massive caseloads. Perhaps because of political pressure and lack of sufficient staffing, the proposed mergers and acquisitions have been, and continue to be, approved without full consideration of the implications regarding the reduction in competition. Thus, millions of U.S. citizens, our people, have been laid off and are out of jobs.   .

Foreign corporations now own many of our vital resource industries, such as transportation, communication and energy. For example, Canadian National Railroad operates in 14 U.S. states; Canadian Pacific Railroad runs its trains through 43 terminals in the U.S. Under the Telecommunications Act of 1996, radio stations may be up to 25% foreign-owned (or more, if the Federal Communications Commission deems it in the public interest). British Petroleum (British-owned) and Shell (Dutch-owned) are among the top five oil companies in the U.S.

When this non-domestic ownership is added to our trade deficit, our bond debt to foreign countries, the outsourcing of manufacturing and jobs to other nations and, particularly, our declining military strength (just 27% of Americans believe the U.S. will be the world's most powerful nation at the end of the 21st century, according to a March, 2010 Rasmussen poll, down from 37% in June, 2009), we have become a nation in jeopardy. Our ability to mount an arsenal of defense, as we did in World War II, has been seriously crippled, and our economic situation is a disaster.

If former presidents Truman or Eisenhower viewed the situation in the U.S. today, they would react with dismay, anger and cleansing action. Eisenhower would not have allowed congress and defense contractors to act like a Good Old Boys' club. Neither president would have allowed the mergers and acquisitions that have taken place in the past few decades.

It is a cruel dialectic that corporations beat their breasts with patriotic fervor, honor the flag, contribute to their communities and then move their business overseas. Likewise, there are many people who only buy the cheapest products available, many of which are manufactured in a foreign country, then complain about the lack of jobs in their communities. In addition, too many citizens find every excuse not to serve in our military, then get angry about the state of our national defense.

When people are hypocritical, whether in business, religion, humanitarianism or patriotism, it weakens our country. Hence, regulation and common sense must be brought to bear.

This book is a call to action. At the end of each section of this book, I put forward several ideas as possible solutions. All citizens of this great country should be forming solutions to our problems. Finding solutions to improve our society is a form of patriotism.

As you would expect, my opinions and philosophies are a product of my life experience, which is greatly varied. During my high school years at a Catholic school, I was actively involved in both sports and academic teams. I also studied for the priesthood, for a time, in a monastery. I went on to receive my Bachelor's degree in economics from Notre Dame University, where I was also involved in sports, debate and politics. I attended Detroit College of Law and finished all but one semester of law school.

As I worked my way through school, I held a variety of jobs, such as grave digger, newspaper columnist, ambulance driver, construction worker, secretary, factory worker, and janitor, among others.

After Notre Dame, I spent three years on active duty and five years on reserve duty as a Marine Corps officer in the 1950s. I went on to work in the marketing department at Ford Motor Company, became Executive Director of Community Affairs for the Catholic Archdiocese of Detroit, and was selected as the first Executive Director of the Metropolitan Detroit Citizens Development Authority (a joint project of Ford Motor Company, General Motors, Chrysler and the United Auto Workers).

Furthermore, I served one term in the Michigan State Senate, where I served on the Appropriations Committee. I later owned a stock-brokerage firm, I handled real estate development, and I spent my remaining career as an independent financial and political consultant to clients that included John Z. Delorean (of concept-car fame) and Matty (M.J). Maroun (owner of the third largest United States trucking company, the Detroit Ambassador Bridge, plus insurance and many other enterprises).

I have devoted a lifetime of work to the Democratic Party. Beginning in my years at Notre Dame, I have been politically active on the local, state and national levels. My experience includes fundraising, precinct work, managing election campaigns and serving on various local and state committees. I was finance co-chair for both Robert Kennedy's and Bill Clinton's campaigns in Michigan.

I believe in fair enterprise, nurturing of invention and innovation, development of the products of invention and innovation and the continued development of new ideas. I do not adhere rigidly to any one specific economic philosophy, but I do believe that capitalism is by far the best economic system. I believe our system of capitalism has become a system of 'moneyism.' I do not believe, as the Wall Street brokers, investment bankers and commercial bankers do, that making money on money (such as stocks in existing companies or derivatives) is an economic stimulator. However, I see very little difference between the two major political parties regarding the outrageous lack of corporate regulation and enforcement.

I envision a United States that gets off the military-industrial complex horse. I envision a United States that through, and because of, its inner strength is able to help other emerging nations and their people. There have been golden ages in the history of man, when peace and prosperity reigned, when there were no wars. I believe this type of society is possible again in America.

People see things through different eyes at different times. My thoughts and proposals are not radical. Rather, I am just suggesting that we learn from our history, that we repeat the successes and correct the mistakes.

As Winston Churchill once said, "The further you look back, the farther forward you are likely to see." He was right on this score.

Part I:
CORPORATIONS WITHOUT BORDERS
GLOBAL TRADE

"When we think of the great power and influence which this country exercises we cannot look back with much pleasure on our foreign policy in the last five years. They certainly have been disastrous years. God forbid that I should lay on the government of my own country the charge of responsibility for the evils which have come upon the world in that period."

—Winston Churchill, *While England Slept*—1938

Trade:(n) the buying and selling or exchange of commodities; (v) to give in exchange or to barter. (*The New International Webster's Dictionary, 2002*).

A basic lesson of economics teaches that there are three essential parts of any business: capital, management and labor. In the past, students of economics were taught that specialization was the central force in a one-world economy. The country that produced the best product would capture that product's market. For example, Switzerland could obtain a majority share of the market in time pieces because its product was superb. Likewise, Germany could become the premier manufacturer of automobiles because of its adherence to quality in the product's manufacturing. In the one-world discussions and writings of the late 1940s and 1950s, those nations that made the best products would succeed, and each nation could find a unique quality-production niche.

These teachings were fueled by a European concept where one should purchase the best suit, best car, best tool and best construction, at the necessary price for that excellence. That may mean buying only one sweater instead of three or one suit every other year, because quality mattered more than quantity.

Today (with perhaps the auto industry as an exception), it is price and not quality that drives the economic engine. Granted, there is a baseline of quality that must be met, but it is not a high benchmark.

Henry Ford, as one of our industrial pioneers, shook the foundations of the early twentieth century corporate world by offering $5.00 a day wages when his competitors were paying their employees $2.00 per day or less. Juxtapose that with modern-day Ford and General Motors, who still pay South African workers a few dollars per day.

The standard of living in third-world countries is significantly lower than we enjoy in the U.S., and I believe that those countries deserve to raise their standard of living just as we once did. But I do not believe the U.S. should suffer from lost employment and a decline in the standard of living in our own country in order to improve the lot of workers in other countries.

Pure, unobstructed, free-wheeling capitalism results in monopolies, elimination of the middle class and, as a result, fewer customers. Neither pure capitalism nor any other economic system will succeed without some necessary controls. In China, the leaders believe their communist government is the only answer, but the country's current success lies in its limited capitalism. China's program will lead to an "oligopoly" – an economic system run by a few people with a few suppliers, which could result in civic unrest or revolution. With the tables turned, similarly, American capitalism without some traffic cops also will lead to an oligopoly.

"Free trade!" is the battle cry of many major U.S. corporations. Yet while proclaiming their patriotism, they have become Corporations Without Borders. While seeking to produce their product or provide their service at the least possible cost, they have outsourced their labor to other nations where costs are lower. If that means closing American factories, cutting off American suppliers, laying off American workers and wreaking havoc on American communities, then so be it. The kicker is that the lower costs are not being passed along to American consumers in the form of lower prices. When I talk about Corporations Without Borders, I am referring to the one hundred or so top revenue-producing American corporations. You can find them in *Forbes* magazine listings (see appendix D).

People can get a sense of Corporations Without Borders by looking at the source of our imports. In 2006, forty-seven percent of our imports were from subsidiaries of U.S. companies that operate abroad, and U.S. subsidiaries of foreign companies. Because of the steep trade deficits, which have grown to more than $4.3 trillion and continue to grow, the U.S. is indebted to foreign corporations.

Corporations Without Borders applauded the adoption in 1997 of the North American Industry Classification System (NAICS), which came on the heels of the North American Free Trade Agreement (NAFTA) in 1994. NAICS replaced the previous system called the Standard Industrial Classification System (SICS), which was established by the U.S. government in 1937 to classify industries by category. Today, under NAICS, it is difficult to isolate production and trade data solely for the U.S. Most of the figures under the new system include data from Canada and Mexico. Curiously, the U.S. Securities and Exchange Commission still uses the old SIC system.

While the trade deficit is hurting American corporations, the U.S. government has its own financial woes. The cost of the wars in the Middle East is staggering. To fund our wars and other spending, U.S. Treasury bonds are routinely sold to other nations and are now held by foreign governments all over the world. Now our government is in debt for those bonds, which adds to our overall economic weakness and puts the U.S. on the road to Third World status.

FREE TRADE?

Because of its trade deficits with almost every major country, the U.S. is sliding toward bankruptcy. Is it because we are importing the very best (thus the most expensive) products, or is it because we are importing products that are almost as good as the product we used to make here, but cheaper because of wage disparity?

When 47 percent of the products being imported are made by U.S. owned-companies located overseas, we are buying the same products that were previously made here by American workers. Corporations Without Borders that send American jobs overseas are tearing at the economic heart of America.

THE AUTO INDUSTRY

The U.S. auto industry's problems are a direct result of two major post-World War II programs: the Marshall Plan in Europe and General McArthur's work in Japan. Both were subsidized by the American taxpayer.

The Marshall Plan was developed to help restore energy infrastructure that the Allied forces had destroyed during World War II. American money and talent were used to rebuild the destroyed facilities; those facilities later enabled Germany to produce cars that were then imported into the U.S. to compete with domestic autos.

In post-WWII Japan, General MacArthur was the effective leader of the country; he undertook the restart of their old economy, transforming it into a model of modern business. This allowed Japan's companies to grow, achieve capital and diversify. One of the areas in which they diversified was automobile manufacturing, and they ultimately became the biggest competitor for U.S. domestic autos and jobs.

In the 1960s, I was the executive director of Metropolitan Detroit Citizens' Development Authority, an organization designed to ameliorate the housing problems during and after the riots in 1967. Walter Reuther, president of the United Automobile Workers, was chairman of our board of directors. Walter Cisler, chairman of the board of Detroit Edison as well as chairman of the Fruehauf Trailer Company and director of some of the country's most revered corporations, was president of our organization. The executive committee included Henry Ford II, Jim Roche, chairman of General Motors Corporation, and Lynn Townsend, chairman of Chrysler Corporation.

Cisler was first and foremost an engineer. Detroit Edison, the company of which he was chairman and CEO, had no competition for electricity in southeastern Michigan. Consequently, he was perhaps somewhat naïve, as I was, regarding the hidden business agendas of others.

Because of Cisler's global connections, I had a rare experience. Cisler had been a leader in the rebuilding of Europe and Japan after World War II, and continued to participate in engineering forums worldwide. He frequently traveled to the Near East and Asia, particularly, Japan. Upon his return from a trip to Japan, Cisler called me to his office for lunch at his desk. Toward the close of the lunch, he told me that some of his friends who were great industrialists in Japan, the Toyoda brothers, wanted to visit Detroit and talk with me about how they provided housing for their workers around their factories. A few days before the visit, Cisler asked if I would be their guide for a tour through the Ford Motor Company Rouge Plant. I proudly conducted the tour, and they were impressed. A few weeks later, a larger group arrived with cameras.

In retrospect, I believe I was used to gain inside knowledge of the most remarkable American car factory of the time—everything was there. A close relationship developed between Cisler and the Japanese leaders. In the late 1960s, one of Cisler's Detroit Edison vice-presidents was named Japanese Consul with a consulate office in Detroit (most other regional consulates were in Chicago). While the U.S. never invaded Japan during World War II, Japan certainly attacked us afterward.

The Japanese car invasion was coupled with the David vs. Goliath assault on the American car industry by Ralph Nader. While a student at Harvard Law School, Nader wrote an article titled "American Cars: Designed For Death." Later, after practicing law and working for two liberal senators, Daniel Patrick Moynihan and Abraham Ribicoff, automobile safety became Nader's personal crusade. His 1965 book *Unsafe at Any Speed,* was highly critical of the American auto industry. Having worked at Ford Motor Co. prior to my election as a state senator in 1964, I was not in complete agreement with everything in the book. Popular belief holds that the book may have gone unnoticed except for the decision of General Motors to investigate Nader, which created a media storm.

Prior to the Japanese invasion or Ralph Nader, the American automotive industry worked very well. Cars looked great, were built and sold affordably, so anyone could buy one (and they did). Admittedly, the cars were not perfect—they rusted easily, for example. Each year, newer gadgets and technology were added so that buyers would be encouraged to buy newer models more frequently.

Was the American car industry of the 1950s, 1960s and early 1970s killed by the Japanese auto invasion or the assault by Nader? No, the car industry helped kill itself by producing a more inferior product.

In 1975, American domestic passenger car production was 6.7 million vehicles and sales were 6.7 million. Imported car sales that same year were 1.5 million vehicles (there was no foreign-car production in the U.S.), and the U.S. automakers did not export any passenger cars (they were manufacturing vehicles in other countries for sale there).

Juxtapose the above-mentioned numbers with those of 2004: the total passenger car production by Ford, General Motors and Chrysler in the U.S. was 2.4 million. Foreign automakers such as Honda, Toyota, Nissan, Mitsubishi, Subaru and BMI manufactured 1.6 million cars in their U.S. plants. New United Motor Manufacturing Inc. (NUMMI), a joint venture between GM and Toyota, manufactured another 237,000 vehicles in the U.S., making a total of just over 4.2 million cars manufactured in the U.S.

Competition from imported vehicles (which includes passenger cars, trucks and SUVs) continues to erode the U.S. supremacy in the industry. In 2006, *Ward's Automotive Reports* reported U.S. sales of all vehicles of slightly over 17 million units. Of that 17 million, almost 11 million were manufactured or assembled outside of the U.S. and then imported for sale, or were manufactured by foreign car makers in U.S. factories. U. S. car makers sold the other 6 million.

The figures in the vehicles sales chart below show how "free trade" has caused the domestic automakers (Ford, GM and Chrysler) to lose almost 5 million vehicles a year to imported vehicles (the increase in imported-vehicle sales from 1975 to 2006).

	1975	2006	Difference
Total vehicles sold in the U.S. (in millions)	8.2	17.0	+ 8.8 million
Total vehicles built in the U.S.	6.7	10.6	+ 3.9 million
Built by Ford, Chrysler and GM	**6.7	6.1	- 0.6 million
Built by foreign makers	0.0	4.5	+ 4.5 million
Total vehicles built outside the U.S. and imported for sale here	1.5	6.4	+ 4.9 million
Built by foreign makers	1.5	3.7	+ 2.2 million
Built by Ford, Chrysler and GM in Canada and Mexico	**0.0	2.7	+ 2.7 million

1975 figures from the 1992 Information Please Almanac. 2006 figures from Ward's Automotive Reports.

** *Some of the 6.7 million vehicles built by Ford, Chrysler and GM in 1975 may have been built in Canada and Mexico, but the source did not list separate figures.*

The U.S. auto companies have always been global. The International Organization of Motor Vehicle Production (OICA) tracks the auto industry worldwide, with data provided by each country's manufacturing association or government. (See Appendix B.) Ford was the pioneer in establishing foreign operations, selling vehicles to the residents of those foreign countries; according to OICA, Ford has production and sales facilities in 19 countries. General Motors has production facilities in 17 countries. Chrysler is producing in only five countries.

OICA also notes that in 2000, U.S. automakers produced almost 13 million vehicles in the U.S. Production fell to about 12 million in 2004. In 2006, before the economic crisis hit the U.S., production was about 11 million vehicles. By 2009, production had plummeted to fewer than six million vehicles.

China produced a paltry two million vehicles in 2000, but in 2009 it became the world leader by manufacturing almost 14 million cars and commercial vehicles. General Motors had no manufacturing facility in China in 2000, yet in 2009 it produced one million vehicles there. Likewise, Ford produced no vehicles in China in 2000, yet in 2009 produced 300,000 vehicles there.

In many foreign countries, U.S. automakers are only allowed to sell vehicles that are manufactured within that country. On the other hand, the U.S. allows foreign manufacturers to sell vehicles here that are manufactured outside the country.

COMPUTERS IN WORLD TRADE

There are remarkable similarities between the evolutions of the automobile industry and the computer industry. Early innovation of automobiles took place concurrently in Germany, France, Italy, England and the U.S., but the production of automobiles soon became the hallmark of the U.S. Henry Ford led the way with Ford Motor Company, which was later joined by General Motors and Chrysler.

Just as man's ability to walk, run and travel were precursors of the automobile, which allowed man to move more quickly and for greater distances, the computer (whose original meaning referred to a person counting) allows man to input, calculate, read, receive and disseminate an incredible volume of information at a vastly higher speed—virtually instantaneously.

When I was a student at Notre Dame University in 1954, my statistics class traveled to Chicago to view the first really giant computer, a now defunct Univac. It seemed to take up an entire city block. It even required a continuous cold-air system to keep the units from overheating. Seeing UNIVAC was like viewing a breathing, mechanical monster.

The innovations in the development of the computer were for the most part an American phenomenon, spurred on by competition with England (as our ally) and Germany (as the real foe). Unlike the development of automobiles, which was a totally free-enterprise operation in the private sector, computers were primarily a result of development by government, universities and other non-profit institutions.

Unfortunately, war and the prospect of war are often the mothers of invention. Computers, as we know them today, were born during World War II, with the U.S. as the focal point of design and innovation. International Business Machines (IBM) developed the first personal computer in 1981. The early leaders of the computer industry were IBM, Remington Rand, Burroughs, and National Cash Register (NCR).

Unlike the computer industry, the automobile industry was a vertically integrated business almost from its beginning. Automobile manufacturers made almost all their own parts and sub-assemblies inhouse, or they were made by wholly owned subsidiaries. Until recently, the only such vertically integrated computer corporation was Apple. That company is now outsourcing some of its parts; but the symmetry of Apple's computer production and assembly has resulted in extremely loyal customers and users, according to a top executive of Best Buy Corporation.

There are seven major hardware components to a computer:

1) mother board
2) central processing unit (CPU)
3) hard drive (storage)
4) memory (RAM) card
5) modem
6) monitor
7) keyboard/pointing device

Component	Total manufacturers	U.S. Manufacturers	Foreign Manufacturers
Motherboards	27	6	21
CPUs	8	6	2
Hard Drives	9	4	5
RAM	26	7	19
Modems	7	5	2
Monitors	21	7	14
Keyboards	18	6	12

Altogether, there are a total of 107 major manufacturers world-wide of the critical hardware components of a computer. There are another 200 sub-manufacturers in the world of the seven critical components. Only 30 of these manufacturers are U. S. corporations.

The following chart shows imports and exports of both computers and computer accessories (resulting in a net trade surplus or deficit.)

	Imports	Exports	Trade surplus or deficit (in millions)
1989	$23,992	$25,214	$1,722
2005	$93,309	$45,536	-$47,773
2006	$101,346	$47,380	-$53,966

Source: U.S. Census Bureau

This dramatic increase in trade deficits occurred over just a seven-year period. In 1989, when PCs were being purchased for the home and education market and the computer industry was beginning to boom, the U.S. computer industry had a trade surplus of $1.7 billion. According to the U.S. Bureau of Labor Statistics, between 1990 and 2006 U.S. computer equipment exports dropped almost 70 percent.

Unlike the automobile, which was being developed simultaneously in several parts of the world, the computer industry was a distinctly American enterprise. So why, in the hardware area, do we currently see so many components made in Taiwan, India, Canada, China, Japan, Korea and many other smaller countries?

Many computer companies, although headquartered in the U.S., have abandoned U.S. manufacturing and assembly. Samuel J. Palmisano, chairman of industry leader IBM, reported that 65 percent of its 307,000 employees were employed outside the U.S. Remember, IBM was a leader in business machines in the United States. In the very early days of the revolution in computer development, it took full advantage of tax incentives and government grants to propel itself to that position, courtesy of American taxpayers via the U.S. government.

Let's take a look at Hewlett-Packard. According to Datamonitor (a database of worldwide business information), HP is the largest global technology company in the world.

A December 2006 article in the *San Diego Union Tribune* by Nicole C. Wong asks, "What is 150,000 minus 45,000? In Hewlett-Packard's world the answer is still roughly 150,000." The article states that Hewlett-Packard (HP) laid off 30 percent of its global workforce since 2002, yet its overall numbers remained unchanged. Where did those jobs go? According to the article, "The global layoffs recently helped HP to chisel away at an expensive workforce in the United States and Western Europe and to funnel work to lower-paid employees in Asia, Eastern Europe and Latin America, said several HP executives in Europe." This method of hiring less expensive foreign workers while laying off Americans is called "churn."

There are several factors to consider regarding jobs that are displaced from the U.S. to other nations. First, considering the cost of living in Taiwan, China, Mexico and India, are the wages paid to those workers sufficient to improve their standard of living, and can these paid workers afford to easily purchase the products they produce? Secondly, what is the disposition of the workers laid off in the U.S.?

When American workers are laid off, bought out or prompted into early retirement, the resulting costs to the U.S. are staggering. Consider these factors: the reduction in taxes that corporations pay on their personnel (FICA); reduction of state and federal revenue from income taxes paid by the workers, and the loss of Social Security and Medicare taxes. If the laid-off worker can no longer afford his home and is forced to go through foreclosure, there is the eventual loss of the property taxes for the local community. His children may have to put aside college dreams because the family had to use all its savings to try to keep its head above water. Subsequently, those children may be ill-equipped to compete in the global economy without a higher education. Finally, and perhaps most obviously, there is the cost of the burden to the government and communities to support these workers and their families when they can no longer support themselves.

On the bright side, the U.S. still remains a major player in the software industry. *Forbes, Software* and *100 Research Foundation* all list the top ten computer software companies, but each publication has different criteria. For example, *Forbes* does not include companies that are also hardware manufacturers, *100 Research Foundation* ranks companies only by sales revenue, and *Software* includes service revenue.

Software	Forbes	100 Research Foundation
IBM (U.S.)	Microsoft (U.S.)	Microsoft (U.S.)
Microsoft (U.S.)	Accenture (Bermuda)	IBM (U.S.)
Electronic Data Systems (U.S.)	Oracle (U.S.)	Oracle (U.S.)
Hewlett-Packard (U.S.)	First Data (U.S.)	SAP (Germany)

Accenture (Bermuda)	SAP (Germany)	Hewlett-Packard (U.S.)
Computer Science Corp. (U.S.)	Google (U.S.)	Symantec (U.S.)
Oracle (U.S.)	Yahoo (U.S.)	Computer Associate (U.S.) (regional HQ in Hong Kong)
SAP (Germany)	Computer Science Corp. (U.S.)	Electronic Arts (U.S.)
Cap Gemini (France)	Electronic Data Services (U.S.)	Adobe (U.S.)
Hitachi (Japan)	Soft Bank (Japan)	Nintendo (Japan)

Dun and Bradstreet, in a 2002 report on software development companies, stated there were 48,242 U.S. companies, employing 580,235 people with gross revenues of $104 billion. The average company workforce was only 12 personnel. The U.S. Bureau of Labor and Statistics reported in 2004 that within the U.S. there were 761,000 software engineers. In 2005, the Bureau also reported that there were 500,000

U.S. personnel classified as computer programmers. When engineers are combined with programmers, the total is approximately 1.26 million.

According to the U.S. Labor Bureau of Statistics for computer software categories (S.O.C. Code #15-1011 to 15-1099), California, the heartland of the computer software business, had 320,000 software personnel in 1999; by 2007 the state had 384,000, a 20 percent increase in eight years.

The computer industry is a highly fragmented business (with the exception of Apple Corporation). Most consumers suffering a computer problem do not have an integrated resource for services or help. Currently, consumers will probably talk to someone in a foreign country when they seek technical assistance. First, there is a barrier of language and connotation. But most importantly, since the greatest purchasers of computer systems are either U.S. residents or U.S. corporations, why is the staff employed by the computer company to give technical assistance not located in the U.S.?

Perhaps we should charge the computer hardware or software manufacturer a fee for every call going to an offshore call center. Some executives might then find it cheaper to hire U.S. residents to conduct their business.

The burgeoning $53 billion trade deficit in the computer industry has been growing, and this is another area where we must put the brakes on outsourcing manufacturing and service jobs, or we will become a Third World nation.

THE UNITED STATES' MILITARY GLOBAL PRESENCE

The history of the world is filled with the tales of military empires: Mesopotamia, Greece, Rome, Spain, France, Great Britain, and more. Many areas of the globe have been occupied or guarded by the military of a foreign country at one time or another. Two of the greatest empires, the Holy Roman Empire and the British Empire, fell for a variety of reasons, but mostly due to exhaustion of capital, labor and management.

Today, American troops are everywhere. Worldwide, the U.S. has 1.65 million military personnel (based on March 2010 Department of Defense data). The breakdown is as follows:

Total Worldwide	1,656,268
Total in U.S. & U.S. Territories	1,127,796
Total Outside U.S. and U.S. Territories	528,472

In Europe	79,675
In former Soviet Countries	127
In East Asia and Pacific	47,339
North Africa, Near East And South Asia	5,826
Sub-Saharan Africa	1,577
Western Hemisphere	2,044
Unassigned	164,484
Iraq (deployed) **	140,100 (rounded)
Afghanistan (deployed) **	87,300 (rounded)

*** As of September, 2010, the number of troops deployed in Iraq and Afghanistan have been shifted, with combat operations in Iraq drawing down, and more troops deployed to combat areas in Afghanistan.*

There are close to 300,000 armed American military personnel perched in non-confrontational areas around the world. According to the same source, Japan hosts more than 35,000 of our troops in warm Pacific waters, and Germany is guarded by more than 52,000 of our finest. Is it for national defense of the United States? Maybe. Is it to protect or secure our country's business interests? Is it a bribe, in the form of economic stimulators to the host countries, in order to assure their friendship? Or is it the U.S. government using our military to protect Corporations Without Borders? This is one result of the military-industrial complex that President Eisenhower warned us about in 1961.

The war in Iraq is an excellent example of our government supporting the interests of Corporations Without Borders, to the detriment of the U.S. The oil companies are the primary examples, and will be discussed later.

If we believe that the invasion of Iraq was based on the idea that Saddam Hussein is evil, then why have we not invaded the countries in

Africa where death and torture occur routinely under villainous dictators like Zimbabwean President Robert Mugabe or Somalian dictator Siad Barre? For that matter, why did we not immediately attack Germany when Hitler was massacring his own people? Clearly, Saddam's cruelty was not the true reason for the invasion of Iraq.

Since the propped-up story of weapons of mass destruction was revealed to be political puffery, it is clear the attack on Iraq was purely and simply about Big Oil. President George W. Bush hails from the state of Texas, where the headquarters of powerful oil companies abound. The oil barons of the U.S., together with their cohorts and partners in Saudi Arabia, are perhaps the most offensive example of Corporations Without Borders.

Saudi Arabia has an enormous interest in the welfare of Iraq and Iran. Iraq and Iran could use the wealth generated from oil militarily against Saudi Arabia for the overthrow of its monarchy. The possibility of the oil wealth funding terrorism is also a factor. U.S. control over the oil industries in Iraq and Iran would benefit Saudi Arabia. Plus, the possibility of the oil industries of the Middle East potentially being under U.S. control must have warmed the hearts of some oil barons.

In its inception and attack strategy, the war in Iraq was wrong. Smart construction contractors soon learn that the more quickly and expediently you build something, the lesser the cost. The construction must be an orderly process. The necessary equipment, building materials and the skilled and unskilled labor must be onsite at the appropriate times. The construction manager must perform like a symphony orchestra conductor to coordinate the project.

Our military equipment and supplies must be the best available, even if it costs us more. Also, we need a troop level of about 300,000 in Iraq and Afghanistan in order to achieve a troop to population ratio of one to 50. This would create a tremendous show of force that, properly deployed, would provide security to the residents and control of the terrorists. Our highest troop level has been about 200,000 personnel. Compare that to the Gulf War, when then-Secretary of Defense Dick Cheney sent 350,000 troops to Kuwait. Why the difference?

Many Americans, while faithfully raising their flags, recounting stories of their forefathers' valorous military service and wearing their patriotism on their sleeve, decry military service as a waste of their time (or of their sons' and daughters' time). And so who ends up serving in the armed forces? With the exception of military school graduates, it is typically the poor and the unemployed. In the past, it also included some lawbreakers who were given a choice by a judge between military service and jail.

Armed forces recruiters cajole and make promises to potential recruits in order to meet their recruitment quotas. They pursue their target recruits with as much zeal as a college football coach going after a high school standout or All-American.

In order to make joining the military attractive, we have focused more on pay and perks than on patriotism. Patriotism is the cloak that hides the primary reason, which is employment and pay. Military pay now starts at $1,447 per month ($17,366 per year) for a newly enlisted serviceman (E-1); with 20 years of service and a rank of E-8, he can make $4,627 per month ($55,522 per year). An officer, as a young lieutenant or ensign (O-1), starts at $2,746 per month ($32,952 per year) and if he climbs to the rank of major (O-4), after 20 years he will make $6,952 per month ($83,424 per year). A full colonel (O-6) with 20 years' service earns $109,152, and a major general (O-8) will earn $151,032 per year, according to the Department of Defense

There are other substantial benefits of military service as well, such as free housing, free food, free medical care, vacation time (30 days per year) and higher education, both while serving and after discharge. Of course, there are retirement benefits after 20 years or more of service, based on the rate of pay upon retirement.

I do not begrudge the pay and benefits for military service to our country. I do regret that every young man and woman is not required to serve our country in some fashion. Some of the life lessons that can be learned in a group environment like the military can be of great benefit to our society. Military service stresses attention to orders, unity and teamwork, personal cleanliness and appearance, maintenance of clothing and equipment, discipline, courtesy, and keeping personal and communal living areas in clean, orderly condition. All this is in addition to combat or other skills developed in the service and carried on into civilian life.

Those in the military receive an education in life and provide a needed service for the country they love. Additionally, many who serve in the military will have an opportunity to travel and make some good friends for life. Obviously, some young men and women may be unsuitable for certain aspects of military service because of medical reasons, but the military should be willing to utilize the skills they have, or help them develop new skills that can be utilized in military service.

The training and responsibility developed during military service prepare service personnel for both military and civilian careers. Unfortunately, the business community does not appreciate, acknowledge or utilize that training, primarily because many business managers have not had the benefit of military service.

The marriage of the military and the industrial complex that President Eisenhower warned us about is in full bloom. The problem with the military-industrial complex is that, with few exceptions, military contractors deal with a Congress and administration whose member shave little military experience. The division between the military and the defense contractors must be clear, distinct, and transparent.

WALMART AND CONSUMER GOODS

According to *Fortune 500* in 2010, Walmart received more revenues than any other company in the world. Its revenues are generated by the sale of consumer goods and food.

"Consumer Goods" includes 26 categories of items that people buy in department stores, gas stations, neighborhood convenience stores, drug stores, etc. The goods range from clothes, televisions and other electronics, to jewelry, china, furniture, pharmaceuticals, toys, etc. This category does not include food, capital goods (real estate, investments, automobiles, and other fungible assets), services or fuel. Consumer goods, with the exception of furniture, are usually small enough in size that they can be purchased and taken home by the consumer without assistance, and they have a limited period of use – that is, they are "consumed" or used to their limit of function.

In 1997, the U.S. exported $91 billion of general merchandise and imported $190 billion, creating a trade deficit of almost $100 billion. In 2006, the U.S. exported $130 billion worth of consumer goods and we imported $443 billion worth of consumer goods. That is a deficit of $313 billion (U.S. Census Bureau of Statistics Part A, Exhibit 7, Import of Goods by End Use Category and Commodity). Consequently, in the years between 1997 and 2006 the trade deficit had grown to 240 percent.

Are the people who are laid off due to corporate acquisitions, downsizing and outsourcing now forced by economics to shop at the Walmarts, Kmarts, dollar stores and other discount chain stores of the U. S.? Remember that the way some discount chains provide cheaper goods is by having them produced in foreign countries, many of which offer meager pay (by U.S. standards) and have minimal or no work standards, such as child labor laws. The more Americans patronize a business that exports jobs to foreign countries, the more we perpetuate the cycle.

Every year, *Fortune* magazine publishes a list of leading U.S. businesses based on revenue (see appendix D). The following chart compares companies in the General Merchandise category (figures are in millions).

	1997	2009
Walmart Stores	$119,299	$408,214
Costco		$71,422

Dayton Hudson/ Target Federated	$27,757	$65,357
Sears Roebuck/ Sears Holding	$41,296	$44,043
Macy's		$23,489
J.C. Penney	$30,456	$17,318
Kohl's		$17,178
Dollar General		$11,796
Nordstrom		$8,627

After a steady increase in gross revenues, in 2009 Walmart eclipsed the next eight companies combined by nearly 58 percent— $408 billion versus $259 billion. Walmart, Costco and Target numbers include groceries, which tend to boost up revenue figures, but historically provide low net income. Walmart claims to have 20 percent of the nation's grocery business.

In the 1950s, the downtown areas and adjacent residential neighborhoods of some of our major cities began to be abandoned. Initially, this was due to the extension of roads, freeways, and utilities (sewer, water, gas, electric and phone lines) which allowed for the development of suburban neighborhoods; new homes with larger lots drew people away from the cities. With the development of these suburban areas came the development of new shopping centers, office buildings and massive school construction.

Unlike early retailers such as Sears, Montgomery Ward, J. C. Penney and Kresge (which later became Kmart) that historically aimed for major markets, Walmart deliberately targeted smaller cities and rural areas with populations from 5,000 to 25,000 people.

In every area where a big-box Walmart or Sam's Club (and to a lesser degree Kmart) store has been built, the downtown areas of adjacent cities have been virtually destroyed. Walmart promises employment, tax basis, charitable donations to the community and— most of all—low prices. The actual result is vacant downtown shops, closed local or regional grocery stores, loss of employment and income, loss of tax base and loss of charitable contributions from the closed businesses.

Thus began the destruction of the heartland of the U.S. and the "Same-ing of America." Regional and local specialties and distinctions have been largely eradicated by national chains that offer the same products no matter where you are. State lines have been blurred and all cities have begun to look the same in the mass-merchandise world.

PROPOSED SOLUTIONS

That which is called Free Trade, in my view, is no trade at all. Perhaps it is a new form of global slavery. It is not unlike the indentured servitude and cheap labor of past centuries. It has the patina of smartness and the heraldry of global economy, but, when stripped of all its smokescreen, it is trading middle and lower class American workers for cheaper, unregulated work forces in other nations. In many instances, we now have to import the same product the U.S. workers were producing.

The U.S. must find a way to bring about fair, balanced trade with each nation.

In order to stop the erosion of the U.S. economic stature caused by debt in one form or other, whether by trade or sale of our treasury bonds, the following solutions are proposed:

1) All U.S. citizens should be studying the U.S. economy. The same attention that we pay to our personal finances should be devoted to learning about how economic systems work, as they have a direct impact on our personal finances. We are conditioned from childhood to expect economics to be boring and complicated, with our energies being directed to leisurely pursuits (like sports, recreation, shopping). We should encourage education about economics at all levels. Those who are educated are in a better position to foster changes in the system and restore long-forgotten basic rules of economics.

2) Let's kick the money arbitragers out of the temple of international trade and fix monetary value. The United Nations should, with studied deliberation, fix the value of each country's currency for perhaps a ten-year period. The value could be set against a mythical U.N. Dollar, taking into account various currency values at a certain date. This would eliminate the portion of the trade deficit that results from fluctuating currency values, and we could then focus on the imbalance of actual product.

3) The U.S. must develop a fair-trade system in which we balance dollar trades. The U.S. or U.N. should publish a wage-to-purchasing power index by trading nations. This is necessary for many reasons. Particularly, what does a dollar wage or its equivalent in South Africa buy in its economy? For example, in my experience, a dinner for four people at a top restaurant during my trip to Johannesburg, South Africa, including steak and drinks, cost about $50, or $12.50 per person. Around the same time, dinner in Chicago or Detroit

would easily cost $250, or $62.50 per person. In other words, an American making minimum wage could buy that meal with about one week's salary, but it would take a South African worker (earning $15 per week) more than three weeks' salary to buy the same meal.

4) The U.S. must develop price equivalency standards on imported goods, particularly those imported from well-developed countries (for example, nations that have national health care programs). Thus, the cost of a car imported from Germany, Canada, Sweden or Japan would include an amount roughly equal to the cost of providing health care to a U.S. employee, added as a tariff or excise tax.

5) We must end our military occupation of Europe, England, Japan and South Korea. Like the old empires of Rome, Britain, Spain and France, we have troops everywhere except where they are really needed. As stated earlier, we have close to 300,000 American troops stationed in about 800 bases in non-combat areas throughout the world. We could use those troops, and the money we are spending to keep them there, to support the American goals in Iraq and Afghanistan, instead of supporting the economies of the European and Asian countries where they are stationed.

6) The North American Free Trade Agreement (NAFTA) between the U.S., Canada and Mexico was a direct blow to the U.S. economy, causing a loss of countless numbers of jobs that left our shores to find homes in Mexico and Canada. It is extremely difficult to determine production and sales statistics for the U.S. alone; because the figures are given for North America as a whole, the U.S. data is blended with that of Canada and Mexico. The statistics may be obtained in *Ward's Automotive Reports*, and even then a reader of the report must have calculator in hand and divide the categories by his own efforts. Do the math. It appears the U.S. automakers now build more passenger cars in Canada than they do in the U.S. NAFTA must be repealed. It was bad in concept and deadly to the U.S. economy in execution.

Part II:
MONEYISM
NOT CAPITALISM

"If size is an advantage, our country should be running wild with dinosaurs. The size of dino's brain was miniscule in relation to their size and that is what is happening to corporate America."

—Jack Farr, Former President of Bank of Flint and former Senior Vice-president of Detroit Bank and Trust (now Comerica Bank)

Some individuals, as part of a larger group of ideologues, believe that capitalism works best without any constraints. "Just get off my back and let me do my own business," cries a financially successful friend of mine. He believes that beating or devouring your business competition is acceptable—no referees are necessary.

Unregulated commerce will end in either a monopoly or a handful of friendly non-competitors, with defeated business owners who were responsible for creating the situation asking for a government bailout. Those who create a problem are rarely the ones willing to fix it.

To many American investors and corporate managers, American labor is fungible. "Fungible" is described in Webster's New World Dictionary: "designating movable goods, as grain, any unit or part of which can replace another unit." In other words, a worker in Mexico or India can replace a worker here in the U.S.

In reaction to my posturing against mergers and acquisitions, my business friends generally remind me that it is a global economy; we compete all over the world, not just in the U.S. Our reward is better stock dividends, and that growth requires suffering. My current "Tea Party" business friends want freedom from government regulations to do whatever they want to do in business.

While it is a truism for Corporations Without Borders to say, "We compete all over the world," it is not true for the average small business. Its competition is the under-priced laborer in Mexico, India, Taiwan or the

Philippines.

I have a long-time friend who is active in the Tea Party movement. He flies around the country to attend their events. He talks about the need for freedom, but he has a hard time giving me specific examples.

One evening in a restaurant, I overheard my young waiter talking to another waiter about the Tea Party. When he returned to my table, I asked his opinion of universal military and community service. His reaction was violently negative. I reminded him about freedom. After his initial reaction, the waiter said he would serve only if the country was attacked. My traveling friend would do the same. As of this writing, neither has served in the military.

When our country was formed, the British theory of capitalism maintained that all capital items—land, means of production and distribution—are privately owned for profit, with concentration of wealth in individuals or in corporations. This interpretation of capitalism caused those without wealth to rebel, leading over the years to Britain's modern socialist/labor state. It went from one extreme to the other. Now the Brits have a government-controlled economy, with aspects of both capitalism and socialism.

What the Corporations Without Borders are espousing is a minimally regulated economic system. Without strong regulations, we will continually cycle through rises and falls of the economy, which destroy savings, capital growth and new business. The past few decades have hopefully provided "master's degrees" to the American public on the consequences of an unregulated economic system.

THE STOCK MARKET

In simple terms, the stock market developed as a way for businesses to raise capital in exchange for ownership, called shares, and a place to buy and sell shares in exchange for cash or other interests.

Traditionally, entrepreneurs or business owners who seek investors basically want three things: 1) sufficient funds to run the company; 2) retention of the most ownership possible and 3) the opportunity to realize the American dream.

Investors, on the other hand, typically look for: 1) return of the capital investment; 2) rise in value of the investment; 3) ability to resell the shares.

Pension funds and managed accounts are the major players in the stock market. Pension Benefit Guaranty Corporation (PBGC), the federal insurer of more than 29,000 U.S. pension plans, covered 44 million people in 2009, according to its annual report. In that same year, there were a total of 78.6 million U.S. workers covered by pension plans, according to the Employee Benefit Research Institute.

An article entitled "Institutional investors boost ownership of U.S. corps to new high" on the website The Free Library.com stated that there were $10.4 trillion in assets under management in pension funds in 2006. In 2009, "Institutional investors – defined as pension funds, investment companies, insurance companies, banks and foundations – controlled assets totaling $27.1 trillion, representing a ten-fold increase from $2.7 trillion in 1980."

With the exception of investment companies which include hedge funds, all of the enumerated entities should or must follow the "Prudent Man Rule." That principle states that those who control other people's money should invest it with prudence, discretion and intelligence with regard to the safety of the capital amount, as well as to income generation.

Here is one of the problems: the stock market and exchange members, usually wealthy capitalists (both American and foreign), enact very few rules to govern their own activity, have minimal requirements for admitting or keeping a company on their exchanges, and provide no corporate management guidelines for selection or continuance. The members of each exchange (stock brokers) purchase their seats to sell the shares of companies listed in the exchange; they can charge what they want for each transaction. The rich and major purchasers pay less for their trades (because of high dollar volumes) than the average investor off the street.

Abuses of the system led up to the Stock Market crash of 1929-30, and resulted in the creation of the Securities Act of 1933, and the Securities and Exchange Act of 1934, which established the Securities and Exchange Commission to provide administrative controls on the market. After the Enron debacle and similar cases of corporate bookkeeping creativity, Congress passed the Sarbanes-Oxley Act in 2002, requiring a public accounting oversight board to obtain correct uniform accountings.

The stated mission of the Securities and Exchange Commission is:

- Protect investors
- Maintain fair and efficient markets
- Facilitate capital formation

But the creation of the SEC did not solve all the problems in the stock market.

In past decades, an executive's average salary was about 26 times the salary of the average worker in the same company. While I worked at Ford Motor Company in the early 1960s, I spent a year or so assigned to the Manufacturing Vice-President's staff. Up and down the hierarchy, supervisors were compensated approximately 10-15 percent more than the staff that reported to them.

Shareholders of U.S. companies, whether individuals or investment-fund managers, seek higher dividends. In search of those cash dividends, shareholders complained years ago about expensive executive "perks," such as the use of company planes for top managers and their families, exclusive and exotic company retreats, memberships in posh clubs and unlimited expense accounts. Companies began to eliminate the perceived perks, but the compensation stealthily reappeared in increased executive salaries, stock options, bonuses and gold-lined severance packages. In 2006, executives averaged more than 600 times the average worker's pay.

Some executives justify their outrageous earnings and benefits by comparing their total compensation to sports personnel who get paid whether they win or lose, which is contrary to the idea of *noblesse oblige*—the concept that privilege entails responsibility. Admittedly, a professional athlete's time and health are severely limited, as opposed to a manager's; but, more importantly, the profitability of the athletic franchise is not the player's responsibility. His responsibility is to play his best for his team.

On the other hand, corporate managers will dismiss the contributions of employees to the success of their companies, but will just as quickly blame the workers for being too costly.

Stock analysts routinely predict the performance of company earnings over a particular quarter. According to *Fortune* magazine, in an article by Stanley Bing, called "Why Your Stock Just Tanked," a consensus of predictions is arrived at through the offices of Thomson Financial, which aggregates all analysts' estimates. If the company's actual performance is less than this consensus forecast, the stock may decline.

Stock analysts a few years out of business school can not only make a million dollars a year, but they can make a given stock rise or fall based on their "expert analysis" of a firm's quarterly report. They are the odds-makers, yet most of them never worked in the industry they are analyzing. Heads can roll in some companies if executive performance doesn't meet the standard set by the analysts. This practice serves no legitimate purpose, unless you believe in crystal balls, and should be stopped.

The fees paid to these analysts and the major brokerage firms for consultation are outrageous, and they have too much power in the marketplace. Their recommendations to buy and sell can cause price swings in a certain stock that, although small per share, can result in windfalls for large investors. For example, if a corporation owns three million shares of a stock and it goes up $0.25 per share, that equals a net gain of $750,000 when the investor sells the shares. The investor can then re-buy the shares when the price returns to normal. For the individual investor, this short-term rise in price may induce him to buy shares of a stock that ultimately will go back down, causing a loss.

The bank bailout program that resulted from the stock market crash in 2008 is just a convenient disguise for another government subsidy program. The crash was a direct result of the neglect by both political parties of the enforcement of current laws and regulation. There are a number of other factors in the crash and subsequent disinvestment. Some of them are:

- The overlapping and integration of banks and investment companies
- Lack of credit standards
- The 1980 Banking Act (which allowed national banks to avoid state banking laws)
- Loss of jobs through mergers and acquisitions
- Movement of jobs overseas, reducing the number of middle class purchasers
- Continual International trade deficits

Basically, the Wall Street gang and their banking cohorts did exactly what they wanted to do, while the U.S. Treasury Department, the Justice Department and the private Federal Reserve looked the other way.

For example, Sandy Weill, the CEO of Traveler's Insurance, wanted Traveler's to buy Citibank in 1998. According to an April 7, 1998 article in the *New York Times*, the law at the time required Traveler's to divest its non-banking holdings within two to five years of the merger. Regarding the legal negotiations with the Fed, Weill is quoted as saying, "We have had enough discussions to believe this will not be a problem." He also said "I don't think we have to spin anything off to make this happen. . .We are hopeful that over that time the legislation will change." The next year, in 1999, he and his lobbyists succeeded in changing the law.

Among the other perceived and real abuses that need to be addressed are:

- Exchange members' compensation makes investment by private individuals too expensive
- Individual shareholders have little voice in company management
- Dividends that should be paid to shareholders are redirected toward other company acquisitions

MERGERS AND ACQUISITIONS

There are four universally accepted elements of any successful business. The four "soldiers" that make a company work are: the innovator, the capital provider, the management and the workers.

The essence of capitalism is that the strongest competitor takes charge of its market by producing better, cheaper or exclusive products, having better management and more creative sales campaigns, or manipulating the market. Cheaper products can be the result of lowball pricing or government price controls. But a common way for companies to manipulate the market in the last 30 years is to buy, merge with or otherwise acquire the competition.

All of the U.S. presidents in the past 20 to 30 years, and their Attorneys General, have allowed mergers and acquisitions that are outside of existing legal parameters. According to a *New York Times* article on December 23, 2006, President George W. Bush's administration approved

32,000 mergers and acquisitions in 2006, worth $3.3 trillion. President George H. W. Bush (1989 to 1993) was the most respectful of the laws regulating this area.

In 1991, when Governor Bill Clinton of Arkansas was running for the presidency, I was very impressed by him; I told my friend, Detroit Mayor Coleman A. Young, that Clinton would be a winner. I quickly raised $250,000 for Coleman to give to Clinton for his campaign. The five donors, which included myself, met with Gov. Clinton in Southfield, Michigan. For 2 1/2 hours the Governor had us, a group of businessmen and lawyers, spellbound. He was not just knowledgeable on every subject, his ken was extraordinary. I ended up on his campaign in the fundraising area, working with Michigan's former Governor Jim Blanchard and Ron Thayer, a fundraiser *sine qua non*.

Despite the excitement of the election, it was the substance of Mr. Clinton's presidency that ultimately brought me sorrow. In 1996, the fifth year of the Clinton administration, it seems as though someone threw a switch that allowed all major acquisitions to take place with our president's blessing. For example, President Clinton approved the merger of Citicorp with Traveler's Group Insurance in 1998, even though the law had not yet been changed. Interestingly enough, Robert Rubin, Clinton's Secretary of the Treasury, resigned and became chairman of the board of Citicorp, for an estimated salary of $15 million, according to Robert Scheer, author of *The Great American Stickup: How Reagan Republicans and Clinton Democrats Enriched Wall Street While Mugging Main Street.*

From 1996 through 2000, there were 26 major mergers and acquisitions allowed. Fourteen were in the communications industry. The total purchase price of those fourteen companies was $637 billion. Nine were banks, and their total purchase price was $289 billion. The remaining three were in oil and gas, at a combined cost of $175 billion.

Communication

YEAR	COMPANY	ACQUIRED BY	COST (in billions)
1996	AT&T Broadband	Comcast	$30.4
1996	Lucent Technologies	Shareholders	$24.1
1997	NYNEX	Bell Atlantic	$30.8
1997	Pacific Teles Group	SBC Communications	$22.4

1998	MCI Communication	World Com, Inc.	$41.4
1998	U.S. Media Group	Shareholders	$31.7
1999	Ameritech	SBC Communication	$72.4
1999	Tele-Communications	AT&T	$69.9
1999	Air Touch Communications	Vodafone Group	$65.8
2000	GTE Corp.	Bell Atlantic	$71.3
2000	U.S. West	Quest Communication	$56.3

2000	Media One	AT&T	$51.9
2000	CBS Group	Viacom	$40.9
2000	AM FM Inc.	Clear Channel	$22.7
		Total	$637.0
		Average	$45.5

Source: 2008 World Almanac

Banks

YEAR	COMPANY	ACQUIRED BY	COST billions
1996	Aetna	Travelers Group	No data
1998	Citicorp	Travelers Group	$72.6
1998	Bank of America Corp.	Nations Bank Corp.	$61.6

1998	Wells Fargo & Co.	Norwest Corp.	$34.4
1998	Associates First Capital	Shareholders	$26.6
1998	First Chicago NBD	Bank One Corp.	$29.0
2000	J.P. Morgan	Chase Manhattan	$33.6
2000	Associates First Capital	Citigroup	$31.0
2004	Bank One	J. P. Morgan	No data

Source: 2008 World Almanac

Oil and Gas

YEAR	COMPANY	ACQUIRED BY	COST billions
1998	Amoco	British Petroleum	$55.0
1999	Mobil	Exxon	$86.4
2000	Arco	British Petroleum	$33.7
		Total	$175.1
		Average	$58.3

Source: 2008 World Almanac

Under President Obama, major mergers and acquisitions of competitive firms have continued unabated, even though the administration initially intended to adhere more strictly to antitrust laws and to slow down the approval rate of corporate mergers and acquisitions. The *New York Times* reported on July 26, 2009, "The more aggressive anti-trust policy was described in interviews with officials at the White House, the Justice Department, other agencies and Congress." The government currently does not have enough manpower to implement the tougher policy.

The history of antitrust legislation goes back to the Sherman Antitrust Act of 1890. One of the stated goals of the legislation was to prevent unions from merging with other unions or forming single associations. This Act also was aimed at the "rape and conquer" conduct of businessmen whose method was to acquire or merge with competing businesses to create a monopoly, and then to raise the prices across the board. The Clayton Anti-Trust Act of 1914 exempted unions from the law and made it clear that monopolies would result from unregulated mergers and acquisitions.

Neither act was intended to rule out the possibility of a company achieving a monopoly by being unique, the best marketer, best planner, having the best price or the best quality. They were designed to prevent the restriction of trade by purchasing competing businesses and eliminating degrees of competition.

Two more antitrust laws were later passed: the I. Robinson-Patman Act in 1935, and the Hart-Scoss-Rodina Antitrust Act in 1976. Taken together, those four antitrust laws provide a controlled version of free enterprise in the United States.

The Columbia Law Review in 1966 Volume 66 stated: "However, the anti-trust laws prohibit not only the exercise of market power, but also its very accumulation. Thus, it is the undesirable accumulation of market power which should be the harm against which the benefits to the community are measured."

On the other hand, the U.S. Attorneys General, from the 1980s until the present, have been almost asleep as mergers and acquisitions ran amok in violation of the antitrust laws. All Americans are paying a price for this neglect. Some of our presidents should have been impeached for allowing huge mergers and acquisitions during their administrations. The trade eliminated by those huge mergers cost America millions of jobs and shareholders were robbed of dividends. Furthermore, the acquisitions required corporations to use on-hand cash and to take on significant debt.

THE COMPUTER INDUSTRY

Caesar said in his famous letter, *"Omnia Gaul est diviso et tre parti"* (All of Gaul is divided into three parts), but he was mistaken—it (France) was one country. People are similarly mistaken about the computer industry. Many think of the computer industry as a single entity, but it is far more complex than that. For the purposes of this book, I will consider hardware manufacture and software development separately (some companies handle both). I will talk mostly about the top companies in each of the two areas.

By many standards, the computer industry is relatively new—it has really only been around since about 1950. The leaders of the developing industry have become saintly icons in the U.S. Investors liked these industrial stocks so much and bid the prices up so high that there was absolutely no relationship between the share price and the book value of the company.

Like many people who grew up without a computer as an everyday necessity or a modern convenience, I viewed computers either as an unnecessary luxury or an awesome research tool. As I undertook the writing if this book, however, my computer became a friend borne out of necessity.

Initially, I intended to address the computer industry only in the section on global economy. I naively believed that this area of mergers and acquisitions did not concern the basement and garage computer companies that grew vertically and were largely self-contained or had friendly suppliers. A partial list of computer companies based on retrievable data from corporate records, *Alacra Stores* and *Forbes2000* indicates how wrong I was.

There have been about 1,000 mergers and acquisitions in the computer industry over the past 20 years.

Company	Acquisitions	Sales Revenue (in billions)
Hewlett-Packard (HP)	197	$115
IBM	107	$104
Microsoft	152	$62
Dell	10	$61
Cisco	146	$40
Intel	63	$38
Apple	25	$33
Motorola	25	$30
Oracle	54	$24
Google	34	$22
Computer Science	18	$17
Arrow Electronics	35	$17

E.M.C.	47	$15
Sun Microsystems	50	$13
Qualcomm	33	$11

In 2010, Oracle purchased Sun Microsystems, thus moving Oracle, with a combined income of $36 billion, to the seventh place on the list.

The top three computer companies (Hewlett-Packard, IBM and Microsoft) are the result of almost 400 mergers. In the cases of Hewlett-Packard and IBM, which were manufacturing calculators and other non-computer equipment, it was probably necessary to merge with computer companies or go out of business. Hewlett-Packard took the money it made in older technologies and invested in the technology of the future—computers.

Amar Mann and Tian Luo, in their January 2010 article "Crash and Reboot: Silicon Valley High-Tech Employment and Wages 200008" published in the *Monthly Labor Review,* indicate the loss of more than 100,000 jobs due to mergers.

According to an article by Nicole Wong in the *San Diego Union Tribune* on December 26, 2006, Hewlett-Packard laid off 45,000 U.S. employees and then hired 45,000 off-shore employees. In 2001, when HP acquired Compaq, a Houston, Texas Co. with 63,000 employees, HP reduced the combined staffs by 15,000 employees. Compaq acquired Digital Equipment Corporation (DEC) in 1998. DEC had more than 140,000 employees, according to its financial report, but because of DECs free-fall, carve-outs and liquidation, it is difficult to determine how many of its employees ended up with Compaq. DEC was subsequently devoured by Hewlett-Packard.

In 1989, HP had acquired Apollo Computer, an early powerhouse. Then, in 1997, Compaq acquired another major player, Tandem Computers. In 2008, HP acquired Electronic Data Systems Corp., with 8,000 employees, and 3COM, with 6,000 employees. With six companies in the fold, Hewlett-Packard is now the top computer company in terms of revenue.

In terms of 2009 net income, here are the top three computer companies:

Company	Percentage Net Income
Microsoft	23%
IBM	13%
Hewlett-Packard	8%

Source: Fortune

In addition to their joint philanthropic efforts, Bill Gates and Warren Buffet have this in common: they both amassed fortunes by acquiring companies. In fact, I was always under the misconception that Gates and his partner Paul Ballmer had built Microsoft from scratch. But, like Buffet ("The Man from Nebraska"), they built it by acquisition. And also like Buffet, they made handsome profits.

With regard to software, the industry is driven mainly by brainpower. It relies more on development and marketing than on material costs, which is mainly for reproduction and packaging of the software.

Many a young computer geek has an idea for a program to make life easier, more entertaining, more educational or better in some respect. But, unless that person has access to a lot of cash, he may end up achieving only nominal success—developing a couple proprietary software programs, with a dozen or fewer employees. Then, he will hope to sell his company to one of the big software corporations for monopoly-like (i.e. millions of) dollars.

Remember the four elements of capitalism? In small start-ups, one person or two may perform all these roles. Innovators are not often good managers, though, and often money providers do not want to work personally. They want their money to work for them. Good managers are goal-oriented and can direct a team of workers to accomplish those goals. The workers execute tasks in the manner the manager and worker agree on.

Imagine this scenario: Eddie B. comes up with an idea that instantly translates any spoken language into another, making it possible for people to travel anywhere in the world and be understood without learning the language. Eddie envisions a microchip containing the translation software that can be purchased and inserted into a cell phone. With the chip in his cell phone, a visitor to a foreign country can speak his own language into the phone and the listener will hear it in his own language.

Now, Eddie has no money, and he has never managed anything, but he's brilliant and motivated. His friend David, who is out of work from his job as a supervisor, wants to help Eddie and knows some investors. With some Internet research and the help of another friend who is an accountant, they develop a business plan. They figure it will take $400,000 to perfect the translation software, produce and market it.

Eddie takes the plan to some of David's investor friends. After visiting several investor groups, they get a pledge for the money and start executing the business plan. Bugs pop up and delays occur. Eddie, as the innovator, wants more time and money to perfect the phone. By now, they are six months behind their expected completion date. The person in charge of marketing and sales wants to get the product into the market, fearful of competition. The investors are anxious for fear of running out of money without a saleable product, and the workers know this means they will lose their jobs.

Finally, they are ready with their first translation microchip for Spanish to English and English to Spanish. They overcame all their obstacles, and the language translation cell phone microchips are a success. Their original business plan calls for them to raise additional capital to increase production and market it more extensively, or to sell the whole operation. Along comes Charlie Company, which is very successful in marketing cell-phone software, and Eddie agrees to sell his company. Eddie receives his well-earned money, and so do the initial investors; the managers receive bonuses or other compensation. But what happens to the workers? Maybe Charlie Company makes the workers an offer to continue working, and maybe it doesn't.

The previous scenario focuses on a small-scale startup company. However, if Eddie B. continued to grow his company on his own, he would eventually capture a share of the market.

While Eddie was developing his translation software, Charlie Company was also developing its own version of translation software, and had already captured 40 percent of the market for that product. Eddie B.'s company had 22 percent of the market. By buying Eddie's company, Charlie Company now has 62 percent of the market.

In that scenario, the government just allowed a merger that

reduces competition in violation of the intent of our country's laws regarding mergers and acquisitions.

When a merger takes place, the following changes can be expected:

- The acquiring company uses its established bank—the bank of the acquired company loses business _The acquiring company retains its existing law firm—the firm of the acquired company loses a large client _The acquiring company retains its existing CPA firm—the firm of the acquired company loses a big account
- The acquiring company continues to rely on its regular suppliers—the suppliers of the acquired company lose business
- The acquiring company places its own managers in key positions, reducing or demoting the management staff of the acquired company
- The acquiring company may or may not be able to employ the staff of the acquired company

At one time, IBM was posturing to buy Sun Microsystems. If that acquisition took place, the lack of competition would hurt three suppliers to both companies, and result in IBM pressing for lower wholesale prices, causing further damage to those suppliers.

In all the cases I've discussed—the fictional example of Eddie and Charlie Company, and the real-life examples—acquisitions will lead to: 1) lack of competition in the marketplace, leading to higher prices for consumers; 2) reduction or consolidation of all types of suppliers; and 3) reduction in employees through layoffs.

The computer industry is young, with perhaps 13,000 computer companies of one sort or another with more than 3 million employees in the U.S. Those numbers will grow if we limit mergers and acquisitions, and also break up the top five companies into smaller competitive companies of about $5 billion to $10 billion each in revenues with equal net income, not allowing them to merge back together again as the phone companies have.

From Table 976 and Table 614 (both 2008) of the U.S. Census Bureau Statistical Abstract of the United States comes the following bad news on the hardware end of the industry.

Computer and Peripheral Equipment
Manufacturing Employment

1990	2000	2006	2007	+/
367,000	302,000	199,000	181,000	-186,000

The loss of 186,000 jobs is a tremendous blow to an economy. Look at the impact of those job losses:

The wages in manufacturing had an average of $21.86 per hour in 2007.

$21 x 40 hours = $840 weekly wages
$840 x 52 weeks = $43,680 yearly wages
$43,680 x 186,000 jobs = $81.2 billion in lost wages

The loss of $81 billion is tragic, but also consider the real impact of that $81 billion. In economic theory, there is a "multiplier effect" of spending—each dollar spent ultimately has the effect of being spent up to 10 more times. When we apply that multiplier effect conservatively, say five more times, that $81 billion amounts to more than $487 billion.

On the software end of the computer business, a totally different story unfolds. While we have lost a great amount of software employment to competitors in Japan, Taiwan and, more recently, India, we have continued to grow, particularly in 2006 and 2007. From Table 596 of the 2009 U.S. Census Abstract "Employed Civilians by Occupation in 2007"

Occupation	2006	2007	Change
Computer hardware engineers	67,000	67,000	0
Computer Scientists and Systems Analysis	715,000	825,000	+110,000
Programmers	562,000	526,000	-36,000
Software Engineers	846,000	907,000	+61,000
Support Specialists	314,000	332,000	+18,000
Database Administrators	99,000	104,000	+5,000
Network and Systems Administrators	180,000	214,000	+34,000
Systems and Data Communication Analysts	356,000	383,000	+27,000
Operations Research Analysts	85,000	87,000	+2,000
Total	3,224,000	3,445,000	+221,000

Where the computer industry is going, I certainly do not know, but if we keep U.S. brains working in the field in this country and then keep the manufacturing production here, it would result in employment gains and other positive economic impact, such as increased Gross National Product (GNP).

Even though Microsoft may have violated antitrust laws by acquiring computer companies to reduce competition, it also acquired companies to integrate innovative systems and products. Bill Gates organized an industry that is providing jobs. In comparison, Warren Buffet has built a large conglomerate of companies in Berkshire Hathaway that were already existing and succeeding in the market; he created nothing. His empire is built entirely from money, not from his own innovation.

THE AUTO INDUSTRY

Growing up in Dearborn, Michigan, the home of Ford Motor Co., provided me with the opportunity to talk with the original Henry Ford on several occasions. Mr. Ford lived a few miles from my school, and in 1941 or 1942, when I was 8 or 9 years old, Mr. Ford would watch us play baseball in the playground after school. Sometimes he would come over and talk to us, usually about baseball, family or grades.

One day, he asked me if I would like to attend his school, The Edison Institute, in Greenfield Village (now part of The Henry Ford). The school was primarily for the sons of Ford executives, friends or business relations. I told him no—not too politely, but emphatically. I told him the kids at the school were stuck up. He laughed.

My father worked more than 33 years at the famous Rouge Plant that in its hey-day had 120,000 workers. I later worked there, in the steel plant and the engine plant.

Everything that was needed to make a car was at the mighty Rouge. Even steel and glass were made there. Some things, but very few, were purchased, such as sand, radios and light bulbs.

The Rouge was the creation of Henry Ford, one man with tremendous drive and intelligence for those early automotive days. Ford combined the mechanical and creative ability of the Dodge brothers, the engineering capability of Walter Chrysler, and the organizational skills of William Durant and the Fisher brothers. In addition, he had the business sense of R.E. Olds, David Buick, Alfred Sloan and the Fisher brothers.

The owners and officers of the various auto manufacturers were friends. Most of them bowled and socialized at the exclusive Detroit Athletic Club. (Sometimes, after a few drinks, the Dodge brothers would start a fight, or so the legend goes.) Consider the fact that Walter Chrysler was, at the same time, both president of Buick Motor Company and vice-president of Olds Motor Company. General Motors is the result of eight major acquisitions:

- Olds Motor Company (Oldsmobile)
- Buick Car Company
- Cadillac Car Company
- Elmore Company

- Chevrolet Company
- Oakland (Pontiac)
- Reliance Trucks
- Opel Cars

Ford Motor Company appears to have purchased only one car company, Lincoln. (Mercury was created as a division of Ford Motor Co. under Edsel Ford.)

Chrysler Corporation acquired approximately 30 companies. The major ones are:

- American Motors (Jeep, Hudson, Nash)
- DeSoto Company
- Dodge Cars and Trucks
- Maxwell (the original Chrysler Company)
- Roots Group
- Stoddard-Dayton Company
- United States Motor Company

This oligarchy was creating the American auto industry as we know it today. In the late 1970s, the wave of Asian imports began. What we have now are almost 2,000 American car companies that did not make it or were forced out by unfair and illegal competition. During my lifetime, there was the Kaiser "Henry J.," the Tucker, the DeLorean, the Studebakers, the Willy's, the Stutz, the Beachcraft, the International Harvester autos and about 20 other would-be, could-be and one-time automobile makers.

All of the 2,000 defunct automobile manufacturers, as well as GM, Ford and Chrysler, were alive and present when GM was being put together in the early twentieth century, when Ford bought Lincoln, and Chrysler acquired a number of car companies.

I could not find a lawsuit or the hint of a lawsuit invoking the Sherman Anti-trust Act or the 1914 Clayton Act when all the automaker acquisitions were taking place. The U.S. Attorneys General were very selective in their prosecution of antitrust cases, because of the extreme caseload, and, in my opinion, the political influence of the perpetrators. In 2004, when the United States sued Oracle to quash the acquisition of

People Soft, the lawyers for the U.S. stated "section 7 of the Clayton Act, as amended, bars acquisitions where in any line of commerce in any section of the country, the effect of such acquisition may be substantially to lessen competition etc." According to this definition, the acquisitions of the automakers in the early days were in clear violation of the law.

The Sherman Anti-trust Act was being used in the very early 1900s to break up banks. Later, in the 1980s, it was used to break up the AT&T/Bell phone companies. Today, those phone companies are coming back together, led by Southwestern Bell, which has acquired several regional Bell companies that were made independent by the break-up.

Today's auto companies are not only too big to fail; they are just too big. At some point, efficiency and profits become lost in bureaucracy. The decision-making process is not conducive for timely reaction to market changes.

For example, in the 1960s when I was at Ford headquarters, if a particular model was not selling as well as forecasted it would start to fill parking lots at the company and at dealerships. It was being assembled with parts coming from all over the country. The field sales people and the assembly plants would notify their division marketing and sales office and the manufacturing staff. The plant labor relations manager would notify the division industrial relations manager. Each one of these division department heads would notify their staff counterparts. The division vice-president general manager would discuss the problem with his staff and the plant manager. The vice-president general manager would decide if it was necessary to cut back production and lay some workers off. He would kick his recommendation upstairs to company headquarters, and so would his staff to their functional bosses at headquarters. Headquarters, labor relations, the legal department and the PR department would all confer. About two weeks would have now expired and the problem would have become worse, with the continuing production of more slow-selling cars or trucks, resulting in inventory languishing on new car lots. The time delay would cost the company millions of dollars in cost and price write-downs.

The decision could have been made at the plant or division level (each plant has a staff that is replicated at every level). The most cost-effective decision-making is at the plant level; the higher up the chain of command, the more expensive the decision-making becomes.

The auto companies should have, and still could be, broken up using any of the antitrust laws that are currently in effect. A break-up would result in smaller companies that would, perhaps, provide a better, more economical product to the consumer, adding more diversity of design and function.

Consider a lineup of individual motor companies that look like this:

- Chevrolet Co.
- Cadillac Co.
- Oldsmobile Co. (bring it back)
- Pontiac Co. (bring it back)
- Buick Co.
- Saturn Co. (bring it back)
- Lincoln Co.
- Ford Motor (includes Mercury)
- Chrysler
- Dodge
- Desoto (bring it back)
- Jeep & Willy's

Instead of three companies there would be 12.

Our government now virtually owns General Motors and Chrysler, so breaking them up could almost be by fiat. If Ford would not divest Lincoln, the U.S. could sue to break Lincoln loose under the Sherman Anti-trust or the successive laws.

Our government could convert their equity to debt. Let all the previous shareholders receive some stock—perhaps one share for every twenty shares—in each new company amounting to a total of 25 percent of the new company. The remaining 75 percent would be sold in the marketplace.

There are a thousand things to be done before the plan could start. A business plan must be developed for each corporation encompassing the needs of each new company, particularly the suppliers.

Now is the time.

OIL COMPANIES

Oil companies are somewhat like whales. They produce oil and they eat smaller oil producers.

Overseas oil companies historically have worked in concert, like a family, rather than sharp competitors. Outside the U.S., most oil companies work to some degree in cooperation with each other, sharing risk and profits.

Inside the U.S., it is a different story. It does not seem that the anti-trust laws have applied to oil and bank companies here, particularly since the 1980s. In 2009, the top three oil companies took slightly more than 70 percent of the entire gas/oil market revenue in the U.S. The base source of these numbers: the companies' annual reports, *Fortune* magazine listing and *The World Almanac and Book of Facts*.

For the top 50 oil companies in 2009, oil revenues in the U.S. were an estimated $2.19 trillion. Even more remarkable, the top three companies claimed almost 72 percent of the revenues. Here is the makeup:

	2009 Revenues
Top Three Companies	$1.57 trillion
Next Seven Companies	$.34 trillion
Next Forty Companies	$.28 trillion
Total	$2.19 trillion

A peek at revenue numbers from 1990 to 2010 might reveal what has happened in the oil business in the U.S.

Revenue (in billions)			
Year	Top Ten Companies	Top Three Companies	Top Three Share
1990	353	274	77%
2005	921	690	75%
2009	1,917	1,574	80%

The top three oil companies by year were:

1990   1) Exxon
       2) Mobil
       3) Texaco
2005   1) Exxon Mobil
       2) Chevron Texaco
       3) Conoco Phillips
2009   1) Exxon Mobil
       2) British Petroleum
       3) Shell Oil

In 1911, President Teddy Roosevelt, after the break-up of Morgan Stanley's Railroad Trust, invoked the Sherman Anti-trust Act to change the powerful John Rockefeller's control and operation of 90 percent of the refined oil business in the U.S. President Taft finished the job. With the concurrence of the U.S. Supreme Court, Rockefeller's Standard Oil Company of New Jersey was broken up into 34 smaller oil companies.

Almost all of those 34 companies exist in some form today. However, through subsequent mergers and acquisitions, most are part of the top 12 oil companies in the U.S.

Wandering through the fields of oil companies is similar to roaming through a field of land mines. Indeed, after World War I, the British government seized an oil company from a German bank (Deutsche Bank) and made it British Petroleum.

Oil and gas people are legendary and are very secretive about their risky business. They spend a lot of time and money figuring out where a field of oil or gas might exist, scientifically estimating the number of feet they will drill before they hit gas, oil or both. What is that drilling going to cost in time, equipment rental (or amortization, if owned), manpower requirements and capital? To complete that cost estimate they weigh expense estimates against their probability of striking oil or gas.

I am not privy to the real inner workings of an oil corporation's brain trust. However, it appears that percentage estimates relative to success are assigned to each new drilling project. A formula then would apply as to how much capital the company wants to risk against the probability of discovery, and based on that assessment, it creates a syndication formula. A high-risk project, where probability of success is only 30 percent, might mean the company will take 35 percent of the syndication and shop the remaining 65 percent to other oil companies or investment bankers. If the risk is lower, such as in a project with a 60 percent chance of success, they will assume a 60 percent stake, and syndicate the other 40 percent.

With the higher potential for success, there appears to be more likelihood of shared participation among the top oil companies, but less participation by the smaller companies.

This syndication system, while it allows different companies to share risk, also lessens competition. The result of this is seen in local gas prices, which are the same among different oil companies. The non-competitiveness becomes apparent when you see two gas competitors on the same intersection with exactly the same prices.

Now compare this situation with other large American business. Take Ford Motor Company's Mustang. As a marketing staffer at Ford Motor Company in the early 1960s, I knew not one soul who would have said "Let's syndicate the Mustang." How about Apple asking competitors to help cover its risks in bringing out the newest iPhone, or Motorola asking competitors to share its development costs in the latest cell phone or communication device. They wouldn't and couldn't.

Since the break-up of the original Standard Oil under the Sherman Anti-trust Act, our Congress has enacted two laws—the Clayton Act and the Hart Rodino Act—making it extremely clear that restraint of competition is unlawful. Apparently, even after the Supreme Court decision to break up Standard Oil into 34 separate companies, there are currently no

Teddy Roosevelts around, nor county prosecutors and state attorneys general with knowledge of the laws or the courage to prosecute.

What the Roosevelt and Taft administrations and the Supreme Court did in breaking up the Standard Oil Trust has been ignored by present-day politicians and the courts. Since the Supreme Court upheld the decision to break up the trust into thirty-four companies, they have regrouped into 10 major oil conglomerates.

Here is what the top 10 oil companies in the U.S. looked like over a 30-year period:

1980	1990	2000	2010
Exxon	Exxon	Exxon Mobil	Exxon Mobil
Mobil	Mobil	British Petroleum	British Petroleum
Texaco	Texaco	Shell	Shell
Standard Oil (California)	Standard Oil (California)	Texaco	Chevron
Gulf Oil	Gulf Oil	Chevron	Conoco Phillips
Standard Oil (Indiana)	Standard Oil (Indiana)	Marathon	Valero
Atlantic Richfield	Shell Oil	Conoco	Marathon
Shell Oil	Conoco	Atlantic Richfield	Sunoco
Continental Oil	Phillips	Phillips	Hess
Phillips	Occidental Sunoco	Hess	Tessoro

Source: Fortune, Forbes and World Almanac

The makeup of the top 10 changed over the years through mergers and acquisitions, which began in the late 1970s under President Carter. Around the same time, President Carter signed the National Banking Act of 1980, allowing the oil companies to charge higher interest rates on their credit cards. How many marriages or acquisitions does it take to make up the top-10 list? Three to four hundred.

Major Oil Acquisitions

Year	President	Company	Acquired By	Price
1979	Carter	Belridge Oil	Shell	$3.6 billion
1981	Reagan	Marathon	U.S. Steel	$6.5 billion
1981	Reagan	Conoco Co.	DuPont	$8.0 billion
1981	Reagan	Texas Gulf	Elf Aquitaine	$4.2 billion
1982	Reagan	CitiServices	Occidental Petroleum	$4.0 billion
1984	Reagan	Gulf Oil	Chevron	$13.3 billion
1984	Reagan	Getty Oil	Texaco	$10.1 billion
1984	Reagan	Superior Oil	Mobil	$5.7 billion
1986	Reagan	Texas Oil and Gas	Marathon	$3.0 billion
1986	Reagan	Mid Con	Occidental	$3.0 billion
1987	Reagan	Standard Indiana	British Petroleum	$7.9 billion
1998	Clinton	Mobil	Exxon	$86.4 billion
1998	Clinton	Arco	British Petroleum	$33.7 billion

1998	Clinton	Amoco-Ohio	British Petroleum	$55.3 billion
2001	Bush	Texaco	Chevron	$43.3 billion
2002	Bush	Conoco	Phillips Petroleum	$24.8

Source: Fortune, Forbes and World Almanac

Company	Number of Acquisitions
1. Exxon Mobil	65
2. British Petroleum America	4
3. Shell	17
4. Chevron	76
5. Conoco-Phillips	35
6. Valero	35
7. Marathon	31
8. Sunoco	25
9. Hess	24
10. Tessoro	10

Source: Fortune, Forbes and World Almanac

Here is the merger and acquisition history of the 10 major oil companies in the U.S.

#1: Exxon-Mobil: Exxon Mobil is comprised of at least six members of the Standard Oil Trust (Prairie Oil & Gas, Washington Oil, Crescent, Standard Oil of New Jersey, Standard Oil of New York, and Vacuum Oil).

The original Standard Oil was formed in Cleveland Ohio by John D. Rockefeller in about 1865. Standard Oil of New Jersey (Jersey) was formed in 1882. In the same year, Rockefeller formed the Standard Oil Trust, made up of many companies including Standard Oil of Ohio and Standard Oil of New Jersey, and he controlled all the oil companies in the trust. Jersey became an independent oil company after the trust break-up of 1911-1914. Along the way, Jersey acquired Imperial Oil of Canada, Humble Oil Company, Anglo American, Monterey Oil, Honolulu Oil, Colonial Oil Co., Washington Oil, a 50 percent interest in Standard Vacuum (StanVac), 48 percent interest in Hunt Oil Co., and finally Mobil Oil. Jersey changed its name to Exxon in 1972.

Mobil was originally Standard Oil of New York, and part of the Standard Oil Trust. After the trust break-up, this orphan grew just as Standard Oil of New Jersey did, acquiring many other companies. The companies purchased included Magnolia Petroleum, General Petroleum, White Eagle Oil, Vacuum Oil, White Star Refining, 50 percent of StanVac, Superior Oil and an increased share of Aramco to 15 percent. After the company was incorporated as Standard Oil of New York, it later became the Socony-Vacuum Corp, then Socony-Vacuum Oil Co. Inc., and in 1955 became Mobil Oil.

Exxon and Mobil merged in 1998. At that time, Exxon was number one, and Mobil was number two in the American oil business. Another way to describe the merger is that Standard Oil of New Jersey married its neighbor Standard Oil of New York.

At the time of the merger, Exxon employed 80,000, and Mobil employed 42,700, for a total of 122,700 employees. Currently, Exxon-Mobil employs 106,100, showing that 16,600 people lost their jobs as a result of this merger.

#2 British Petroleum (BP): BP was created out of the Anglo-Persian Oil Co. in 1914 when the British government gained majority control of the company. As the victor in World War I, BP acquired the

European Petroleum Union, with its excellent refinery process.

In 1969, BP made its first entry into the United States oil business with the acquisition of 25 percent equity stake in Standard Oil of Ohio (Sohio). It became a major owner (53 percent) of Sohio in 1978 and 100 percent in 1987.

BP acquired Amoco (Standard Oil of Indiana) in 1998 and purchased ARCO (Atlantic Richfield) in 2000. Sohio acquired Solar Refining Company.

Amoco (Standard Oil of Indiana) acquired or formed Pan-American Petroleum, Amoco Egypt Oil Co., Amoco Sharjah Oil Co. and Amoco Oman Oil Co.

ARCO (Atlantic Richfield Oil Co.) is the result of the mergers of Atlantic Oil and Richfield Oil. Prior to that merger, Atlantic purchased Hondo Oil. Together, they acquired Sinclair Oil, Anaconda Oil, Tricentral and Union Texas Petroleum Holdings. In 1998, a subsidiary of ARCO called Western Midway Co. exchanged properties in California with Mobil Corporation. Western Midway was sold to Vastar Resources, a public company created by ARCO in 1994. ARCO is major shareholder of Vastar.

#3 Shell Oil: Royal Dutch Shell, the parent of Shell Oil, entered the U.S. in 1912 with the creation of the American Gasoline Company. Shell Company America was formed in 1915. Shell Co. acquired Mexican Eagle, merged with Union Oil Co. of Delaware and purchased Belridge Oil.

#4 Chevron: Chevron's beginnings go back to 1879 with the formation of the Pacific Coast Oil (PCO) in the San Francisco area. The Standard Oil Companies of New York and New Jersey shipped oil from the east coast, and from Standard Oil of Iowa, to the West Coast, creating severe competition for PCO. Eventually, PCO merged with other west coast Standard Oil companies into Standard Oil of California, formed by Rockefeller, which became independent in the 1911 break-up.

Standard Oil of California (Chevron) discovered oil in Saudi Arabia. Chevron and Texaco formed Caltex to develop and market the greatest oil production. In 1944, they formed Arabian American Oil (Aramco). Standard Oil of New Jersey and Ohio became partners. In 1980, ownership of the fields reverted to the Saudi government, but Aramco still operates the fields under contract.

In 1961, Chevron acquired Standard Oil of Kentucky, which had previously acquired Reed Oil Co. In 1984-85, Chevron acquired Gulf Oil, which had been founded in 1901, and had acquired Paragon Oil in 1929 and Warren Petroleum 1955. In 1988, Chevron purchased Tenneco's oil and gas reserves in the Gulf of Mexico. In 2001, Chevron acquired Texaco, which was originally formed by the merger of Red Star Oil Co. and Texas Oil Co. in 1911. Texaco subsequently purchased Indian Oil Co., McColl-Frontenac Oil Co., Paragon Oil and Getty Oil (which had itself previously acquired Tidewater Oil). The Gulf Oil and Texaco mergers were the two largest acquisitions at their time. Gulf was $13.2 billion and Texaco was $43.3 billion. In 2005, Chevron acquired Unocal (Union Oil of California) for $16.8 billon. Unocal began in 1890 with the merger of Hardison & Stewart Oil, Torrey Canyon and Sespe, then later acquired Pinal-Dome and Pure Oil Co.

#5 Conoco-Phillips: Originally Continental Oil Co. (Conoco), it was formed in 1875 and became part of Rockefeller's Standard Oil Trust. In 1929, Conoco merged with Marland Oil and Rocky Mountain Oil (also a Standard Trust member). In 1981, it was purchased by E.I. DuPont de Nemours and became a wholly owned subsidiary. Conoco merged with Phillips Oil in 2001, which received almost 57 percent of the new combined company. Phillips was originally formed in 1917 by Frank Phillips.

#6 Valero Energy: Valero was created in 1980 as a spin-off of Coastal States Gas Corporation. Through a series of refinery purchases, Valero became the largest refiner in the U.S. in 2005. Its acquisitions include: Basis Petroleum in 1997 (refining), and Paulsboro, New Jersey Refinery in 1998, Ultramar Diamond Shamrock in 2001 and Premcor Inc. (refining) in 2005. In 2000, Valero acquired from Exxon one refinery and 350 gas stations.

#7 Marathon Oil: The Ohio Oil Company started in 1887, was purchased by Rockefeller two years later, and was ultimately separated with the Standard Trust break-up. Ohio acquired Transcontinental Oil Co. in 1930. Transcontinental used the product name "Marathon" to indicate speed and longevity. In 1962, the name of Ohio Oil Co. was changed to Marathon Oil.

Along the way, Ohio Oil Co. (Marathon) purchased Transcontinental Oil, Aurora Gasoline Co., Plymouth Oil, Pan Ocean Oil, properties of Husky Oil, Pennaco Energy, Khanty Mansiysk Oil, Marathon

Ashland and Western Oil Sands Inc. In 1948, Marathon joined Amerada Oil and Conoco to form the Conorado Petroleum Co. In 1962, it formed the Oasis Group with Amerada Hess and Conoco to discover a major field in Libya. And in 1998, it formed Marathon Ashland Petroleum LLC with Ashland Inc., incorporating elements of refining, transportation and marketing.

#8 Sunoco Inc: With the incorporation of Keystone Gas Co. in 1881 by Joseph Newton Pew and Edward Octavius Emerson, another American Horatio Alger story began to unfold. In 1889, these tycoons created Sun Oil Co. In 1895, Sun Oil bought out Merriam & Morgan. It later acquired Lone Star & Crescent Oil Co., Sunray DX, Exeter Oil Co., Victor Oil Co. properties, Atlantis Petroleum Corp. and Philadelphia Refinery from Chevron. In 1998, the corporation officially changed its name to one of its brand names, i.e. Sunoco. Incidentally, in 1904, Sun Oil brought the first commercially successful asphalt to market.

#9 Amerada Hess: This company was established in 1919 by British Lord Cowdray. Over the years, it acquired Goodrich Oil and Cameron Oil. In 1948, Amerada joined Continental Oil (Conoco) and Ohio Oil (Marathon) to form Conorado Petroleum, and later purchased Conoco & Marathon's interest in Conorado Petroleum. In 1964, Amerada joined Marathon, Conoco and Shell to form Oasis Consortium. It then acquired Ashland Oil. In 1969, Hess Oil purchased stock of Amerada and became Amerada Hess.

#10 Tessoro: In 1964, Tessoro became a spin-off of Texstar Corp. Its acquisitions include Elmore Petro Co., Sioux Oil Co., 50 percent interest in BP-Trinidad-Tobago, S & N Investment gas stations and Digas Co. gas stations. In 2000, Tessoro formed Mirastar Co. and contracted to operate filling stations at Walmart stores.

The myriad mergers in the oil industry are like the tentacles of a greedy, black octopus – they are so twisted that no one can determine where they begin, but ultimately, they end up in your wallet.

BANKING

Banking in the U.S. has undergone major changes since the 1970s. The very nature of banking as a simple depository of funds in the form of savings and checking accounts has changed drastically. With the 1980

Banking Act (which virtually destroyed states' usury laws), the Reigle-Branch Banking Act in the early 1990s, and the repeal under President Clinton of the Glass-Steagall Act banking took a turn for the worse (see Appendix C).

These changes allowed banks to invest in unstable securities, such as hedge funds, commodities markets and venture capitalism.

USURY

In the 1950s, my saintly, All-American brother had his law license suspended for two years for a violation of the Michigan Usury Law. He was the closing attorney for a mortgage company that somehow charged slightly over the interest rate limit then existing in Michigan. In another case, Ben Levinson, owner of Michigan Mortgage Co. and a prominent member of the Democratic National Committee, went to jail in the 1960s for illegally providing the required down payment for a home in order to qualify the buyer for a Federal Home Loan mortgage. Back then, most mortgages required a 20 percent down payment, which was considered an indication of the purchaser's credit-worthiness. Today, no such down payment requirement exists.

Today, a lender can charge a credit card holder any interest rate it chooses. Furthermore, in an inverse logic, lenders charge customers with poor credit history higher interest rates than those with better credit history. So, if you struggled to pay bills in the past, lenders are going to make sure you continue to struggle. The same scenario applies to home and car insurance. Are these charging higher interest rates for people of lower income an outward manifestation of our nation's religious and civic posturing? I believe these practices are morally offensive.

The most profitable aspect of the credit card business is the "catch-22" user. Fictional Eddie B. is an average consumer with an average credit score. Slam Bang Oil Co. sends Eddie a new credit card with a $500 limit, and it is a MasterCard, which can be used just about anywhere. Eddie pays his bills on time for six or seven months, but he has edged closer to his $500 limit. Slam Bang sends Eddie a letter announcing it is increasing his credit limit to $750. A few months later, the same scenario occurs: Eddie is pushing his credit limit, and Slam Bang raises his credit limit to $1,200. A year later, Eddie's up against the limit again. Slam Bang, generous to a fault, increases his limit to $2,000. By this time, Eddie's credit card balance consists of maybe $500 in principal—i.e. stuff he bought—and $1,400 in interest. All things being equal, Eddie could be at fault for not controlling his spending in relation to his income. But until we make sure all Americans understand basic economics, Eddie is not solely culpable. Until Congress passed the Credit CARD Act of 2009, Eddie's monthly payment would go first to interest and then to principal. But the interest on the unpaid balance continues on its usurious path, with rates as high as 37 percent.

A report of the Internal Board of Governors of the Federal Reserve Report (as printed in the 2009 *U.S. Census Bureau Statistical Abstract*) in 2004 stated that 24 percent of family credit card holders "hardly ever pay off the balance." If you do not include credit card holders over age 55, the percentage who hardly ever pay off their balance is much higher. The same report indicates that there are another 20 percent who sometimes pay off their balance, and 56 percent who almost always pay off the balance. The latter group has been decreasing while the former group has been increasing. The study was over the 10-year period from 1995 to 2004. A current study including the most recent recession of 2007-08 would be even more enlightening.

The culprit is the Depository Institutions Deregulating and Monetary Control Act of 1980. That was President Carter's poison pill to small businesses, the middle class and the poor. The Act allowed national banks to charge any interest rate on instruments of credit. The deluge of high rates followed and became one of the triggers of the 2007 financial meltdown; greed ran rampant through the land, but mostly with the 'money changers' in New York's financial district.

Free enterprise and capitalism are necessary and desirable, but we need criminal regulation to shackle those who cry for free enterprise, then destroy it through their greed and abuse. Laws with tough consequences governing these money-changers are needed to kick them out of the temple we call the United States. They may be domestic companies or foreign; it makes no difference. These credit-crunching snakes are eating our own. The U.S. cannot tolerate the gluttony of the banking community—on Wall Street or throughout the country.

THE GREAT DEPRESSION

Many believe that the Great Depression was caused by failures in our unregulated financial system. Consider some history that led up to the Crash of 1929.

The Panic of 1893, which was precipitated by railroad overbuilding and shaky financing, resulted in bank failures and a run on gold, depleting the U.S. Treasury. In 1895, J.P. Morgan loaned the U.S. Treasury more than $60 million dollars in gold to stabilize the country's credit worthiness.

By 1902, however, President Theodore Roosevelt's Attorney General brought suit under the Sherman Antitrust Act against railroad conglomerates, which included J.P. Morgan as an owner of Northern Securities Company. The suit resulted in the break-up of the conglomerate into independent companies, including (among others) The New York Central, The Pennsylvania Reading, The Chesapeake and Ohio, and The Northern Pacific.

In 1907, another panic occurred as a result of a drop in the stock market and caused a series of bank failures. J.P. Morgan, who was still allegedly frustrated by the break-up of his railroads, stepped in with a pledge to shore up the banking system with his own money and arranged mergers with solvent banks, restoring "good faith" in the U.S. Treasury. In exchange for saving the banking system, Morgan extracted a commitment from the U.S. government not to invoke the Sherman Anti-Trust Act against the banks (as they did on his railroads), perhaps setting a precedent. I believe that Morgan also worried that if he did not stop the run, it might become a tidal wave and kill his own banks. This panic ultimately resulted in the creation of the Federal Reserve System in 1914.

In the 1920s, investors had bought stocks on margin, with up to 90 percent borrowed money. As stock prices began to decline in 1929, it became more difficult for investors to repay their loans. The situation escalated throughout Wall Street until the Crash of 1929. As headlines screamed about stock failures, ordinary citizens caused a run on the banks as they tried to save their own money. Because the banks could not recover their loans to investors, they could not pay their depositors. This resulted in many bank failures.

In 1930, 1,352 banks bit the dust; another 565 failed in the next 50 years. But in the 1980s and early 1990s, thousands of banks went under. The Federal Deposit Insurance Company reported the following bank failures:

President(s)	Years	# of Bank Failures
F.D. Roosevelt	1934-1941	370
FDR/Truman	1941-1952	30
Eisenhower	1953-1960	20
Kennedy/Johnson	1961-1968	35
Nixon/Ford	1969-1976	65
Carter	1977-1980	45
Reagan	1981-1988	1,480
G.H.W. Bush	1989-1992	1,286
G.W. Bush	2001-2008	55
Obama	2009-	140

What changed to cause such a tidal wave of failures? As I mentioned previously, the Depository Institutions Deregulation and Monetary Control Act of 1980 is one of the worst banking acts in U.S. financial history. Not only did it take away from the states the right to set meaningful usury rates, but, somewhere along the way, the Federal Reserve and the Office of Thrift Management increased the amount of loans an institution could make with a similar deposit (reserve) requirement. Many institutions, particularly in the Savings and Loan sector, approved risky loans without enough reserves to cover loan defaults.

When President Carter signed the 1980 Act, there were approximately 15,000 banks in the U.S.; today there are about 7,500. As shown in the list above, bank failures account for about 3,500 of the reduction. What happened to the other 4,000? The answer, as in so many other industries, lies in destructive mergers and acquisitions. Like the "Pac-Man" of video game fame, the banks ate each other— some ate so many they became "Too Big to Fail." The first Too Big to Fail was the Continental Illinois National Bank and Trust in 1984, which was at one time the U.S.' seventh largest bank. Its failure resulted from bad loans to oil producers and drillers, loans to their investors and bad loans purchased from a failed Oklahoma bank. News of that bank's failure caused Continental's depositors to withdraw $10 billion in deposits in May of 1984. The FDIC poured in $4.5 billion and saved the bank. But, unable to find buyers, the FDIC was forced to operate the bank until it was bought by the Bank of America a full 10 years later.

On April 22, 2010, NBC reported six big banks, which together had accounted for 17 percent of all bank deposits in 1995, now controlled 63 percent of all bank deposits in the United States.

What makes a bank too big to fail? How did some banks become so big that we, the taxpayers (through our government), have had to bail them out? The answer is that every president since Jimmy Carter has neglected prosecuting any violations of the laws regarding mergers and acquisitions. Somehow, the regulators—i.e. the Treasury Department, FDIC, Office of Thrift Management and the inept Federal Reserve—do not believe that banks should be subject to these laws. Many papers, books and articles have been written about whether or not U.S. banks are subject to this country's antitrust statutes. Whatever the conclusion, it is true today that no anti-trust violation actions have ever been brought against banks.

Before the days of mega banking, commercial loans commonly involved several participating banking institutions. For example, a business customer in Michigan, say an automobile dealer, applied to Detroit Bank and Trust for a commercial loan of $5 million. Detroit Bank and Trust (DB&T) issued a commitment to fund the loan. DB&T either funded the loan by itself, or it asked other banks to participate—both to share the profits and the risks, and also to maintain good business relationships with its fellow community banks. DB&T took a large portion of the loan, and divided up the balance with several other banks (a local syndicate). The points, interest and other details were agreed upon by the members of the syndicate.

This also happened on a national level. For example, suppose Ford Motor Co. went into its long-time local bank, Manufacturers Bank, and needed a $100 million loan. Manufacturer's was comfortable at the $15 million level; so it went to New York City to its correspondent bank, Chase (the Rockefeller bank). Chase took on another $36 million, and syndicated the balance of the loan.

This system of sharing risk through a syndicate of both local and national banks was appropriate to protect the deposits of individual banking customers.

The simple essence of American banking up to 1980 was that banks could take its customers' deposits, add them to its equity, and make loans in multiples of that amount according to bank laws and regulations.

Contrast that with banking after 1980. State usury laws are ignored. Banks can issue credit cards and charge any interest rate they want. The final blows to U.S. residents came during the Clinton Administration with the Riegle-Neal Act, which allowed for nationwide branch banking; the Gramm-Leach Act, which blurred the separation between investment and commercial banking; and the repeal of the Glass-Steagall Act, which removed all barriers between investment and commercial banking. When interviewed on "Meet the Press" on April 18, 2010, Clinton said the repeal of the Glass-Steagall Act was inevitable, because it legalized what was already happening. He was referring to the steady weakening of Glass-Steagall provisions by more recent banking legislation. (See Appendix C.)

Those actions resulted in our current banking situation, in which banks are now far more than just depository institutions. They are involved heavily in investment banking, insurance, stock brokerage, hedge funds and many other exploits that put deposited funds of individual bank customers at greater risk.

Of course, they are still banks, so they jump up all the fees and create new ones. The one I despise the most is the fee my bank (which pays me no interest on my checking account) charges individuals for cashing checks I have written to them. Another common bank practice is the service fee on ATMs for cash withdrawals. The fee for each machine is a standard amount, not a percentage of the amount withdrawn. If the fee is

$2.50 and you withdraw $20.00, you are paying 12.5 percent of the $20.00; with a $3.00 fee, you are paying 15 percent. A smart ATM client may only need $20.00, but will withdraw $100.00 in order to reduces his cost to 2.5 percent or 3 percent.

"TOO BIG TO FAIL"

Through mergers and acquisitions, publicly traded banks grew to massive proportions as they swallowed up smaller banks and competitors. A real-life example involves ABN-AMRO, a Dutch bank holding company; ABN-AMRO purchased an old Chicago bank named LaSalle, and in Detroit, ABN-AMRO purchased Standard-Federal and Michigan National Bank. One could correctly argue that ABN-AMRO's purchase of LaSalle did not diminish competition. However, the same standard does not apply in Michigan, as two competing banks became part of one banking conglomerate. ABNAMRO in the U.S. grew to $107 billion in assets.

The examination of the top six banks in the United States (both for assets and revenue) will reveal banking "Pac-Man."

Bank	2008 Revenue (in billions)	Bank	2008 Assets (in billions)
Bank of America	$113.1	Bank of America	$2,800
Citigroup	112.3	J.P. Morgan/Chase	2,200
J.P. Morgan/Chase	101.5	Citigroup	1,900
Morgan Stanley	62.2	Wells Fargo	1,300
Goldman Sachs Group	53.6	Goldman Sachs Group	850
Wells Fargo	51.7	Morgan Stanley	770

Source: Fortune, Federal Reserve

The years 2008 and 2009 witnessed changes in the complexion of various banks. Wells Fargo more than doubled its assets from mid2008 to December of 2009, with the acquisition of Wachovia, a much larger bank. Morgan Stanley became a bank holding company. A four-year comparison of the top five banks (by revenue) indicates that the big banks, despite being hurt by the economic storm of 2008-09, were not broken.

Revenue (in billions)	2006	2007	2008	2009
Bank of America	117	119	113	121
Citigroup	147	159	112	91
J.P. Morgan/Chase	100	116	101	109
Goldman/Sachs	?	88	54	45
Wells Fargo	48	?	52	29

Source: Fortune and World Almanac

Three of these banks—Bank of America, J.P. Morgan/Chase, and Wells Fargo—are the repository of just under one third (31.5 percent) of all the bank deposits in the United States. Taking the top five together, their assets are more than $8 trillion. Here's a look at the top 50 U.S. Banks in assets:

Ranking of banks	Total Assets
1-5	$8.0 trillion
6-10	2.5 trillion
11-15	1.0 trillion
16-20	750.0 billion
21-25	569.0 billion
26-30	350.0 billion
31-35	292.0 billion
36-40	179.0 billion
41-45	110.0 billion
46-50	72.0 billion

(Source: Federal Reserve)

After the first five banks with combined assets in the neighborhood of $8 trillion, the next 45 of the top 50 banks have combined assets of slightly less than $6 trillion.

A similar pattern holds up when looking at the top banks by revenue. In 2004, the top three banks took in revenues of $228 billion. The next seven banks had revenues of $126 billion. In 2006, the same top three banks had revenues of $364 billion and the next seven banks took in $166 billion.

Whether by assets or by revenue, the figures indicate the "Pac-Man" bankers are getting bigger.

But of course, these are bank holding companies, whose primary business comes from ownership not only of commercial banks, but also of other commercial businesses, such as brokerage firms, investment banks, insurance companies, credit card companies, and other small operations (which I like to refer to as "fiddle farts"). Bank holding companies can even invest in sinful hedge funds, where managers sell sometimes rotten-smelling items and with cherubic faces claim they are the newest perfume. As a bard would say, "Therein lies the rub." The bank holding company is the newest money changer.

How did those banks and their parent holding companies get so big? With hundreds of mergers and acquisitions. Here's what I found for the years 1982-2009.

Bank/Bank Holding Co.	# of Acquisitions
J.P. Morgan Chase	433
Citigroup	304
Bank of America	298
Wells Fargo	147

Source: Alacra Stores

It takes a big appetite to become Too Big to Fail, but the banks are only partly to blame. The government, by neglecting prosecution of antitrust violations and through congressional actions removing protective barriers, has had a hand in creating the monsters that they are then bound to rescue, leaving taxpayers on the hook.

The government and the banking community have a great responsibility to the American public to chart a safe course for individual economic security. That obligation mandates a much higher degree of oversight.

MEDIA

Newspapers in the U.S. are privately owned and they print whatever they choose. Television and radio stations operate under grants for use of the public airwaves, which are valid for a certain number of years. Throughout the duration of the grant, the broadcaster is required to report the usage of the broadcast time by category—i.e. scheduled programming, commercial advertising, free public service announcements, etc. At the conclusion of the grant period, the public is able to protest the misuse of the grant.

In recent years, the amount of time devoted to commercial advertising has grown from three minutes per half hour to eight minutes per half hour. Government advertising was initially free, since the "public" owned the airwaves. Our government now pays for advertising minutes. The Federal Communications Commission (FCC) has acted generously toward the grantees (broadcasters). This applies to both the advertising minutes and also the ownership of multiple media outlets or stations within the same market.

The media's treatment of news leaves a lot to be desired in terms of depth of coverage and neutrality. A good example of the lack of depth is the coverage on both the health care reform legislation and the financial reform legislation in 2010. In the past, both newspapers and broadcast stations had reporters who specialized in topics, and often understood the subject in more depth than the legislators, thus being able to educate the public about the facts; today, we get regurgitated sound bites. When there were actual investigative reporters behind the sound bites, the news was often more meaningful. But many newspapers have eliminated the true investigative journalist, mainly because of budget concerns. Along came cable television and the Internet, and we now have a huge selection of shallow news sources, but very few sources of probing, analytical reporting.

The newspapers are out of the reach of government's control. But cable television, both wired and over the air, uses public rights of way and airwaves which may be regulated by the government.

PROPOSED SOLUTIONS

The stock markets must reform themselves; if they are unwilling, then legislation should follow to control their members and their listed companies.

Reports on all transactions from stock analysts with buy or sell recommendations should be filed with the SEC to prevent damage to small investors from market fluctuations.

The range of commissions and transaction fees should be standardized, with a smaller range between volume players and mom and pops.

Amendments to tax laws should make it easier for companies to compensate their executives with "perks" and awards without severe tax liabilities. This would allow companies to reduce new executives' salaries and stock options to a ratio that is more fair to the shareholders and common workers.

Corporate executive compensation limits should be at the prerogative of the board or stock exchange. Compensation should be based on a fair range of all companies in the same or similar business. Most companies have a salary range for each position. The salary range for top corporate executives should be based on profitability. Stock awards or bonuses should also be based on profitability, and it should not be based on just the immediate year but over a set period of time.

This would prevent the scenario of an executive who works diligently to make his division or company profitable and establishes the tools of success, yet does not see immediate results in the form of higher profits. If he is subsequently fired by an impatient board of directors, this opens the door for the next executive to realize the success made possible by his predecessor, and enjoy the kudos, bonuses and promotions to follow.

The antitrust laws regarding mergers and acquisitions must be upheld more consistently. Congress should provide the Department of Justice with the proper tools, including appropriate fines, to enforce existing antitrust laws, and encourage the Department to deny proposed mergers that fall outside legal parameters.

If caseloads remain too high for the department staff to handle, the federal government should contract with outside law firms to handle the cases.

Large conglomerates should be broken up to better serve the marketplace by providing more competition and better efficiency. Banks of more than $50 billion in assets (as a result of mergers and acquisitions) should be broken up into smaller entities.

Each oil field should be independently owned and operated by a single oil company. Oil syndicates that are created to pool risk, but which also lessen competition, should not be allowed.

Oil and gas competition in the U.S. should be limited to domestic (U.S.-owned) corporations. This would lessen our dependence on foreign entities in the event of conflict or war.

For strategic reasons, Shell and BP, because of their foreign ownership, should be asked to leave the country. Their refineries and properties should be divided in a competitive manner and sold to smaller U.S. companies.

Exxon-Mobil, Chevron, Conoco-Phillips and Valero should be broken up. The result would be about 35 companies with the revenues of a little over $50 billion (in U.S. dollars) each in 2010.

The recently passed Financial Reform Act of 2010 is a small beginning, but the good portions that once again would have separated commercial banking from investment banking were deleted from the final version. An amendment to the bill in the Senate, which would have limited commercial banks to investing a maximum of three percent of their capital in risky ventures like hedge funds, was eliminated to secure the Judas vote of the freshman senator from Massachusetts. His vote ensured no cloture (debate) could take place.

So, our combined or unified banking system can secure other people's money and risk it according to the latest "in vogue" investment program.

We need a constitutional amendment that limits commercial banks to depository accounts, individual and commercial loans, and that also limits investments of the capital of the commercial bank to the Glass-Steagall Act of 1933.

Citizens should call for this constitutional amendment and put that question—are you for or against such an amendment?—to every candidate for every state house seat or U.S. Congressional seat.

All broadcast media—television, cable radio, satellite—should require their news personnel, both on and off the air, to have a minimum of two years of post-secondary education in journalism, English, history and simple mathematics. Opinion commentators should have direct background experience in the fields in which they render their opinion. Editorials by the owners or producers should automatically allow for rebuttal.

License grants should provide for only one license per grantee per geographic area or market. License grants should be limited to a set period of years, and after expiration be open for bids.

Commercials should be run for only three minutes of every half hour of programming. One additional minute may be used for public service announcements and government advertising, which should be aired for free. Looks and age should not be major factors in filling on-air staff positions.

Enlisting these strategies can result in millions of saved jobs and a stronger economy.

Part III:
AN UNHEALTHY HEALTH INDUSTRY

"The health of the people is really the foundation upon which all their happiness and all their powers as a State depend."
—*Benjamin Disraeli*

"The health of nations is more important than the wealth of nations."
—*Will Durant*

In searching for an appropriate title for this chapter, I interviewed more than a dozen individuals in the health industry. I asked them to describe in one word the health industry. Receptionists and entry-level staff, who were thankful to have a job with health benefits, described it as wonderful. Administrators and other mid-level staffers, such as nurses, described it as complicated or burdensome. Doctors described it as broken.

Very few people are happy about the state of U.S. health and medicine. Our industrialist and business leaders decry the cost of medical insurance and are cutting their costs or not offering it. Hospitals and providers of health care complain that the health insurance industry cuts their reimbursements too deeply.

The drug industry, while spending millions on television and print advertising, argues that the cost of drugs in the U.S. is predicated on immense research requirements.

Doctors grumble that, after spending nine or more years in post secondary education to study medicine and medical specialties, they are told by an insurance company administrator not only what medicines to prescribe and treatments to offer, but how much they should get paid for their services. Consider also that, while an administrator may have only spent four years in college, many doctors are more than $200,000 in debt by the time they receive their degrees and licenses.

Health insurance providers, while constantly escalating premiums, carry impressive surpluses. Their bottom line increased even more after the passage of Medicare Part D (prescription drug benefit), which is provided for by federal law, but is sold through private insurance companies.

The current cost of health care in the U.S. is approximately 16 percent of our gross domestic product. With the 2008 GDP of $14.265 trillion, that means we spent almost $2.3 trillion on health care. According to *Forbes*, other industrialized nations with government-paid health care spend much less (as a percentage of GDP), such as Canada (10 percent), United Kingdom (8.4 percent), Japan (7.9 percent), Germany (10 percent), China (4.5 percent) and India (4.9 percent). How can we compete with the products of other nations when our products are priced to include the cost of our U.S. health care? We must get the cost off the corporate books and onto the government books and simultaneously reduce health care costs.

MEDICAL INSURANCE

In 2006, U.S. residents paid almost $800 billion out-of-pocket expenses for hospital care, doctors, dentists, nurses, therapists, prescription drugs, home health care, nursing home care, non-durable and durable medical products, and personal health items. Medicare and Medicaid spent $970 billion, and private insurance doled out $723 billion for its insured customers. Finally, another $155 billion was donated, written off or provided by private corporations.

Out of Pocket	$800 billion
Private Insurance	$723 billion
Medicare and Medicaid	$970 billion
Donated	$155 billion
Total	$2.65 trillion

Source: Statistical Abstract of the United States

If we take those figures and apply them to the approximate number of people covered in each area, we get the following results:

	Population (millions)	Expenditure (billions)	Average expenditure Per person
Privately Insured	200	$723	$3,615
Medicare and Medicaid	81	$970	$11,975
SChip (children)	7	$6	$857

Source: Statistical Abstract of the United States

The 2010 health care reform is a step in the right direction, but it does not come into full effect until 2014. Unfortunately, it does not take the onus off corporations competing against companies from countries like Canada, Germany, Japan, China and other economies with government or socialized medical care. Our corporations must add the cost of employees' health premiums to the prices of their products. In order to compete on price, they move operations out of the U.S., where they do not have to pay the cost directly. It is paid through taxes. We suffer loss of jobs. It does not make any economic or rational sense. Some in our society call a national, public or government health program "socialism." It is the opposite. It allows our companies to compete with foreign competitors, and it may save and/or return jobs to the U.S.

Insurance coverage is also a factor of where you live. The top 10 states for percentage of uninsured population are:

1)	Texas	(24%)
2)	New Mexico	(21%)
3)	Florida	(20.3 %)
4)	Arizona	(19%)
5)	Oklahoma	(18.7%)
6)	California	(18.5%)
7)	Louisiana	(18.5%)
8)	Nevada	(18.3%)
9)	Mississippi	(18.1%)
10)	Georgia	(17.6%)

The 10 states that have the highest percentage of insured population are:

1)	Minnesota	(91.5%)
2)	Hawaii	(81.4%)
3)	Iowa	(90.7%)
4)	Wisconsin	(90.6%)
5)	Pennsylvania	(89.8%)
6)	Rhode Island	(89.8%)
7)	Massachusetts	(89.7%)
8)	Connecticut	(89.6%)
9)	Michigan	(89.4%)
10)	Ohio	(89.3%)

Interestingly, when the states with the highest uninsured population are compared to unemployment rates, five of the states were significantly below the national unemployment rate of 5.5 percent; three were near the national rate and two were above it.

Of the top 10 insured states, all but one showed significant increase in unemployment rates from June of 2007 to June of 2008. Rhode Island, at 7.5 percent, increased by 2.5 percent; Michigan, at 8.5 percent, was the highest in the nation.

One might conclude that the states with the greatest number of insured residents are unionized industrial states, which makes the cost of doing business higher than for states with fewer unions (thus fewer insured residents). Is it more cost-effective to relocate your corporation where total employment costs may be less, causing unemployment to grow in states where costs are higher due to employer paid insurance premiums?

Medicaid, i.e. government-supported medical coverage, correspondingly has increased across the country since 1984 by about three percent, with the largest increase in the south by almost six percent. Current estimates, according to the U.S. Census Bureau, are that 53 million U.S. residents do not have any insurance in 2010; they cannot afford private insurance and they make too much money to qualify for Medicaid.

The health insurance providers, both private and government, dictate the covered or reimbursable amount for any medical procedure or prescribed medicine. Because of limited payments allowed by insurance companies, the internal medicine, family practice and other non-surgical doctors have to increase their patient load. Twenty or thirty years ago, doctors would see one patient in 15 to 20 minutes. Today, one of my doctors schedules three people every fifteen minutes, resulting in long waits for patients, sometime hours. These physicians must increase the number of patients and procedures to make up in volume what they are losing in reimbursements, and some have lowered the standards of necessity for visits, procedures, surgeries, etc.

How did the once-powerful medical lobbies let this happen? Could anyone imagine a U.S. Congress full of lawyers allowing the regulation of their private practice fees by a third party?

One of the capital sins of the health insurance industry is the multiple cost system. The announced or stated cost of services by health care providers is only the cost for uninsured patients. For insured patients, the stated costs are fiction. Every insurer establishes what it will reimburse a provider for the procedure, visit, service, surgery, hospital stay and number of hospital days allowed. Insurers also tell which medications are allowed (i.e. that they will pay for), regardless of what doctors feel is best for the patient.

In 1998, cancer discovered my prostate gland. The treatment, which involved radioactive pellets, ended up curing the cancer but burned a hole (fistula) in my colon, through the prostate and into the urethra. The result has been twelve operations, dozens of visits to ten different doctors, several long hospital stays and many invasive procedures. When this ordeal began, I was not yet 65, was insured by Blue Cross-Blue Shield and paying about $1,100 in medical premiums per month, plus my deductible and co-pay. I became eligible for Medicare A & B in 1999 (thank God!).

I sued the hospital and doctor on the basis of malpractice and won in a settlement. I was informed by an honest lawyer that I must now repay Blue Cross-Blue Shield and Medicare for the portion of my care that they paid. The stated cost for all my treatment was more than $500,000. What Blue Cross and Medicare actually paid the providers was about $129,000. That's the amount I then paid back to Blue Cross and Medicare.

"Self," I said, "I don't get it." I paid premiums each month to my insurers. I fought the initial phase of the case without a lawyer; I beat my opponent's lawyers and their motions. My insurers were not in the courtroom with me and they were not at the settlement conference with me and my lawyers working on an hourly basis. They were not in the hospital with me, subject to repeated surgeries and procedures. But they were there with their hands out after the battle. My insurers ended up paying nothing for my care, but I never got any refund of my premiums. I don't get it.

The insurance industry and the banking lobbies are the two most powerful untamed political powers in the U.S. Remember when the lobbyists for Traveler's had the laws changed (retrospectively) to facilitate its purchase of Citicorp?

Consider the Medicare Prescription Part D program, which was a windfall for the private health insurance companies, but limited coverage for recipients. Insurers with their powerful lobbyists had all of their mouths, plus their hands and feet, in the trough.

Hospitals must also deal with the insurers. A former vice-president of marketing for one of the Blues informed me about how the insurance company's bean counter would sit down each year with the hospital's bean counter and allocate reimbursements for the year. The Blues' beaner would point out that the hospital had been averaging 250 insured appendectomies a year, for the last three years. Blue would offer to pay $800 per operation for the year and write the hospital a quarterly check for $50,000. The hospital would say in response "We can't do it for $800 anymore, all our supply costs have increased; we need $900 per operation." The two settle for $850 per operation and move on.

It sounded pretty fair to me, but I am told they don't do it that way now.

Today, it seems the only criteria are the cheapest costs to the insurer. At the same time, insurers do not act with the same cost-effectiveness when dealing with their own friendly, long-term suppliers. Every vendor of medical supplies or services trying to get new business with medical insurers (particularly the Blues or self-insured union or government medical programs) has a difficult task. As in every field, long-term relationships between suppliers and purchasing agents are cultivated at conventions, entertainment or sports events. These vendor relationships should be conducted at arm's-length, but some become cozy business partners.

The preferential treatment goes both ways. The boards of directors of health insurance companies are populated with directors from the companies for which they provide management services through a self-administered health program. This opens the door to potential, and costly, conflicts of interest.

PHARMACEUTICALS

It is difficult to determine exactly how much is spent annually in the U.S. by private industry on pharmaceutical research and development (R & D) (see appendix E). The National Institutes of Health (NIH) reports that it awarded $41 billion in research grants for R & D in 2009. The private pharmaceutical industry spent about $65.3 billion on R & D in 2009, according to PhRMA. The numbers for R & D spending aren't always easy to pin down—in 2006, the figures from three different sources give three different figures:

Pharmaceutical Executive	$76.1 billion
Research America	$64.5 billion
PhRMA	$58.8 billion
Average	$66.6 billion

The total amount spent on R & D for drugs in 2006 appears to be:

Private Sector Average	$66.6 billion
National Institute on Health (NIH)	$15.0 billion (est.)
Private States, Universities	$13.7 billion
Total	$95.3 billion

More than $95 billion was spent on treating one form or another of illness and disease, not on curing them. Diphtheria, polio, malaria and measles are just some of the diseases that have been nearly or completely eradicated. But what about heart disease, cancer, diabetes and the hundreds of other health problems?

Research America makes the following statement in its 2006 report on expenditures on R & D: "We estimate the amount of money spent on research to improve health to be around $116 billion. The amount is less than six percent of the $2.1 trillion spent on health in the United States in 2006."

However, when you analyze the detailed spending in its report, it shows that not all of the government research spending (through the NIH) is done for human research. Some of the funds are directed to the Department of Agriculture for animal research, and some toward the Department of Defense for chemical and biological warfare. So the $15 billion listed in the chart above for NIH is inclusive of those funds. If you take only the amount spent on human research, the number is closer to $12-13 billion.

The private sector represents about three-fourths of pharmaceutical R & D. Often, that research results in a drug with little hope of recouping the money spent to develop it, because the market for the drug is so small. For example, if only a few thousand people in the U.S. have a rare disease like phenylketonuria (a metabolic disorder that, if untreated, can lead to brain damage), the market for a drug to combat the disease would be too small for a major drug company to justify the money spent on R & D.

In order to ameliorate this situation, Congress enacted the Orphan Drug Act in 1993. The act provides for the FDA to allocate money for private research and development of the drug. The act also provides the researching institution a 50 percent tax credit, waivers of user fees, and exclusive marketing rights. Since the Act took effect, more than 250 drugs have received broad marketing authorizations, and more than 1,100 different drugs have been approved for limited use.

Another obstacle to R & D is the time it takes to develop a drug, go through FDA approval and get it to market. The R & D of a safe, health-restoring and marketable drug now takes 9 to 15 years. According to PhRMA, up to 10,000 different compounds may be tested in the first phase of research to arrive at 250 combinations that may solve a medical problem. In the second phase, those 250 combinations will be reduced to around five through rigorous testing, and in the third and final phase, FDA approval may result in one approved medication.[1] The FDA claims it cannot approve or disapprove a drug in ten months.

_____

1. PhRMA

RESEARCH

Pre-discovery

Goal: Understand the disease and choose a target molecule.
How: Scientists in pharmaceutical research companies and government, academic, and for-profit research institutions contribute to basic research.

5,000–10,000 Compounds

Discovery

Goal: Find a drug candidate.
How: Create a new molecule or select an existing molecule as the starting point. Perform tests on that molecule and then optimize it (change its structure) to make it work better.

Preclinical

Goal: Test extensively to determine if the drug is safe enough for human testing.
How: Researchers test the safety and effectiveness in the lab and in animal models.

250 Compounds

DEVELOPMENT

Investigational New Drug Application

Goal: Obtain FDA approval to test the drug in humans.
How: FDA reviews all preclinical testing and plans for clinical testing to determine if the drug is safe enough to move to human trials.

Clinical Trials

Goal: Test in humans to determine if the drug is safe and effective.
How: Candidate drug is tested in clinical setting in three phases of trials, beginning with tests in a small group of healthy volunteers and moving into larger groups of patients.

5 Compounds

Phase 1	Phase 2	Phase 3
20–100 Volunteers	100–500 Volunteers	1,000–5,000 Volunteers

New Drug Application

Goal: FDA reviews results of all testing to determine if the drug can be approved for patients to use.
How: FDA reviews hundreds of thousands of pages of information, including all clinical and preclinical findings, proposed labeling and manufacturing plans. They may solicit the opinion of an independent advisory committee.

Manufacturing

Goal: Formulation, scale-up and production of the new medicine.

One FDA-Approved Drug

Perhaps this is naive, but why can't this process be streamlined? How quickly, accurately and safely might scientists with modern equipment, computers and scientific tools at their disposal isolate 250 compounds for the second pre-clinical stage? What if hundreds of scientists worked on the same medical problem—not physically together, but in concert?

It is interesting to note that two pharmaceutical companies are in the top 100 companies on the *Fortune 500* list (see Appendix D). Pfizer, at number 40, makes an impressive 17 percent profit on its total revenues; and Merck at number 85, earns a whopping 47 percent profit!

MARKETING

The Public Library of Medicine published "The Cost of Pushing Pills: A New Estimate of Pharmaceutical Promotion Expenditures in the United States" in April of 2008. The report was authored by Marc-Adne Gagnon and Joel Lexchin. The report states:

". . . with estimates based on the information in the annual reports of ten of the largest global pharmaceutical firms, . . . between 1996 and 2005, these firms spent a total of $739 billion on marketing and administration. In comparison, these same firms spent $699 billion in manufacturing costs, $288 billion in R & D and had a net investment in property and equipment of $43 billion, while receiving $558 billion in profits."

In their annual survey of members (2008 Table 1), PhRMA indicated R & D worldwide was at $237.8 billion for the same 10-year period (1996-2005). This is a difference of $50 billion. (The difference in data from one source to another is typical, as indicated earlier, and makes it difficult to precisely tell the whole story.)

The U.S. buys 70 percent of the drugs manufactured in the world. In order to make doctors and patients aware of their drugs, pharmaceutical companies use marketing techniques, such as:

- seminars
- entertainment
- office and hospital promotions
- medical journal advertisement

- direct to consumer advertising
- free samples
- kickbacks or bonuses to doctors

Seminars or small meetings with doctors and medical staffs may number as many as 400,000 in a given year. Some include meals and entertainment, which could consist of dinner at a top-rated restaurant for doctors (plus spouses or dates), cocktails and a Broadway-like show.

Pharmaceutical sales people are legendary. These peddlers are bright, and they know their products. In reality, they may be the modern day equivalent of the old bottle waving medicine men selling elixirs in early America. The difference is the variety of the products; some of the modern drugs are about as effective as snake oil.

During my medical ordeals of the last several years, I have spent many hours in doctors' waiting rooms; the pharmaceutical sales personnel are always there. They are handsome men and lovely women with ever-present smiles, occasionally delivering lunch or another treat for the doctors and staff, and—of course—drug samples.

In my numerous hospital stays, I have viewed merchants of meds rolling in carts of food and other treats for the staff, in exchange for their subtle agreement to promote their products, which include not only drugs but medical devices.

Traditional advertising of a particular drug product in medical or science journals is intended to induce a doctor to prescribe the product. This differs from direct to consumer advertising, which includes radio, Internet, direct mail, magazine, newspaper, billboards and television ads. This type of advertising is designed to convince consumers to ask their doctors for the drug. Fine print notwithstanding, few consumers are able to determine, on the basis of advertising, what drug may be suitable for their situations.

This type of promotional spending is not quantifiable, but has been the subject of much examination in the press, particularly in the prestigious New England Journal of Medicine, the Public Library of Science and many of the journals for medical specialties.

The controversy over advertising began in 1996 when the FDA permitted direct-to-consumer advertising by drug companies.

Initially, the FDA was a watchdog in issuing violations of drug advertisement regulations. However, citations have dwindled, as Julie M. Donohue, Marisa Cevasco and Meredith Rosenthal pointed out in their August 2007 article in the New England Journal of Medicine. The paper, entitled "A Decade of Direct to Consumer Advertising," stated "violations . . . fell from 192 in 1997 to only 21 in 2006." Oversight seems to be less stringent than ever, judging by the explosion in the number of drug ads in recent years.

For those who doubt that direct-to-consumer advertising is effective, how about the practice of doctors giving free samples to patients? First, the patient loves the doctor for giving them. They're free! But ultimately, the patient has to pay for the drug if he decides to continue using it. There are a lot of great doctors who routinely provide samples to their poorest patients. Some doctors also provide samples to insurance covered or uninsured cash-paying patients. But the motives for giving the free samples are important. Are the samples given for:

- concern for the patient's inability to pay?
- immediate resolution of a health problem?
- marketing of the drug?
- improvement of the doctor-patient relationship?

Pharmaceutical companies may also provide direct incentives to doctors for writing a great number of prescriptions for their products. A legal reward might be an "educational" cruise for doctors, with lectures on new procedures or products. But the whole area of incentives from drug suppliers walks a fine line between legal and illegal.

The borderline of illegal rewards to doctors was reported on by New York Times health writer Gardiner Harris in June, 2004. Harris reported he interviewed twenty doctors to "shed light on the shadowy system of financial lures that pharmaceutical companies have used to persuade physicians to favor their drug." He wrote that doctors had received checks from the Schering-Plough Pharmaceutical Company, for up to $10,000 per check.

The article stated that a federal investigation was in process, and most of the major drug companies received subpoenas for records. Harris wrote, "At the heart of the various investigations into the drug industry marketing is the question of whether drug companies are persuading the doctor, often through payoffs, to prescribe drugs that patients do not need or should not use or for which there may be cheaper alternatives."

(My call to the Boston FBI office on August 29, 2008 to inquire about the status of the investigation was turned aside as an agent informed me that I had to file a Freedom of Information Act request. My lawyer, Mayer Morganroth, has filed many FOIA requests in many different cases without success, which doesn't inspire much confidence in the system.)

In June 2007, Gardiner Harris and Janet Roberts wrote in the *New York Times* about doctors being paid to conduct clinical trials in Minnesota, the only state requiring disclosure of payments to doctors who had been disciplined by the State Board of Medicine.

The article stated, "The timed examination of Minnesota's trove of records on drug payments to doctors found that from 1997 to 2005, at least 103 doctors who had been disciplined or criticized by the state medical board received a total of $1.7 million from drug makers. The median payment over the period was $1,250; the largest was $479,000."

The ever-persistent Gardiner continued exposing shady practices. In June, 2008, writing with Benedict Carey, Gardiner again reported in the *New York Times* about questionable practices in drug research. The article reported on Senator Chuck Grassley's (R-Iowa) investigation of grants from drug makers to university drug researchers.

Gardiner and Carey reported on the financial magic of Dr. Joseph Biederman, Dr. Timothy E. Wilens, and Dr. Thomas Spenser. In response to an inquiry from Sen. Grassley, the trio of Harvard researchers reported receiving combined payments from drug companies (called income) of $2.6 million from 2000 to 2007. This income came in the form of consulting fees from the drug makers and was not disclosed to the university, which was also receiving research grants from NIH.

A rational person reading this article might come to a number of conclusions. The first might be that drug companies have found a legal form of inducement through NIH grants, supplemented by their own corporate generosity, helping researchers (doctors) to push the pencil and promote their product.

The second might be that the NIH looks the other way on potential conflicts of interest by institutions receiving their grant money.

The third is that universities, like Harvard, consciously overlook unethical or questionable practices for fear of losing noted researchers like

Dr. Biederman. Compare that inaction to a bar owner who looks the other way when a popular bartender occasionally dips into the till or provides drinks to a friend. The questionable practice may ultimately generate greater revenue to the bar (or university).

Perhaps the best thoughts on the subject of drug marketing were in a paper entitled "Doctors and Drug Companies," in the *New England Journal of Medicine*. The author, Dr. David Blumenthal M.D., M.P.P., stated, "When a great profession and forces of capitalism interact, drama is likely to result. This has been the case where the profession of medicine and the pharmaceutical industry are concerned. On display in the relationship between doctors and drug companies are the grandeur and the weaknesses of the medical profession, its noble aspirations and its continuing inability to fulfill them. Also on display are the power, social contributions and occasional venality of a very profitable industry etc. . . ."

The following is a summary of the mount of growth in marketing expenditures compared to R & D.

	1996	2004	Increase
Research and Development	$13.3 billion (U.S. Census Bureau)	28.6 billion (U.S. Census Bureau)	113%
Marketing and Advertising	$11.4 billion (INS Health reported in NEJM)	$57.5 billion (Public Library of Science)	404%

THE HOSPITAL INDUSTRY

In the years 2004 and 2005, the American Hospital Association reported that U.S. hospitals had a constant of 35.2 million inpatient visits each year, which boils down to about one in five U.S. residents (including about 10 percent repeat visitors). Even more striking is the number of emergency room visits. About 114 million patients visited U.S. hospital emergency departments in 2005, or one out of three residents.

To say hospitals in the U.S. are a major industry is a gross understatement. In 2005, there existed a total of 5,756 hospitals. Community hospitals—the ones where babies are born, surgeries take place, pneumonias get cured and people die—comprise 4,836 of the total or a little over 84 percent. The community hospitals are broken down into (a) non-governmental non-profits (60 percent); (b) for-profit hospitals (18 percent); and (c) state and local government hospitals (22 percent). There are 226 federal hospitals for U.S. employees, retirees and veterans. A hospital is an artificial body that metaphorically has the attributes of a human body. It has a brain (doctors, administrators and nurses); it has a nourishment system (food, medicine, fluids); it has a eproduction system (maternity and surgery); it has a cleansing system (the laundry, baths and showers); and it renews itself (maintenance, modernization, and rehabilitation).

Hospitals have undergone changes in the past 28 years both in total number of hospitals and number of beds per hospital. My observations are that big hospitals (800-1,000 beds) are downsizing and small hospitals (under 100 beds) are either remaining the same, becoming "feeder" hospitals in a larger system, or becoming larger due to area population growth. Here is the statistical comparison between community hospitals in 1980 and 2005, as reported in the *Statistical Abstract of the United States* (2008 & earlier editions):

	1980	2005	Change
Number of hospitals	6,965	5,756	-1,209
100-plus Beds	3,755	2,942	-813
Fewer than 100 Beds	3,210	2,814	-396
Admissions per 1,000 population	159	119	-40
Average length of stay (days)	7.6	5.5	-2
Outpatient visits (per 1,000 population)	890	1,976	+1,086
Outpatient visits (in millions)	263	673.7	+375
Surgical operations (millions)	18.8	27.5	+9
Surgeries per admission	0.5	0.8	0.3
Emergency room visits (millions)	82.0	118.9	+37

The 1969 Webster's Seventh New Collegiate Dictionary's definition for hospitals is: 1) a charitable institution for the needy, aged, infirm or young; 2) an institution where the sick or injured are given medical or surgical care. The 2002 Webster Pocket Edition defined a hospital simply as a building or location for the care of the sick and injured.

In the U.S., few charitable institutions for the needy exist anymore, with the exception of veterans' homes. The aged, if necessary, are cared for in their own homes, in their children's homes, in private, expensive for-profit nursing facilities or, if poor, by the Sisters of Charity. The mentally infirm are sometimes in resident institutions, whether private or public, but many live with their families or in adult foster homes. Health insurance limits the number of inpatient days that are covered by the policy. You must have virtually no assets to qualify for Medicaid coverage for nursing home care.

I am no stranger to hospitals. I have had many close encounters with this intergalactic phenomenon, with about 25 inpatient stays for everything from back surgery to cancer. I can't even count the number of outpatient visits. I have been fortunate enough to be a patient in the hospitals of seven different states: Michigan, Florida, North Carolina, Washington, Missouri, Ohio and Virginia. I have been in both government and non-profit hospitals, but never in a profit-driven hospital, except for outpatient procedures.

I've had some interesting conversations with four different hospital administrators over the years, regarding the continuous dialogue they have with insurance companies, auditors and financial staffs.

For any one service a hospital performs and for which it bills a patient, there are four scenarios under which the hospital will be paid different amounts. The hospital submits a bill to the patient at a certain dollar amount for the service. In scenario one, the uninsured patient is expected to pay that amount in full, either up front or on a payment plan. In scenario two, if the patient has private insurance, the insurance company will pay the hospital in an amount considerably less than the billed amount, because of something called "diagnosis related groupings" (DRG). The amount of reimbursement for each type of procedure is usually set by the insurer. In scenario three, if the patient is covered by Medicare, Medicare will pay an amount more than a private insurance company but still less than the amount billed. Here is an example off one of my bills:

Provider	Date of service	Type of service	Charge Amt.	Medicare approved	Medicare paid	Your portion
Doctor Y	1-3-08	Surgery	$2071	$626.29	$501.03	$125.26
Doctor Y	1-3-08	Surgery	$1118	0.00	0.00	0.00
		Totals	$3189	$626.29	$501.03	$125.26

This bill was for arthroscopic surgery on my knee. Medicare approved just under 20 percent of the total charges billed and paid just under 16 percent of the charges. I paid the other 4 percent with the $125.26 co-pay. I did have supplemental insurance, but it did not pay the $125.26 because I had not reached my deductible. So, of all the charges billed, the hospital makes out with about 20 percent, and must write off the rest.

In scenario four, if the patient has Medicaid, the hospital will be paid at a slightly higher rate than for either private insurance or Medicare. Medicaid reimbursement is slightly higher than Medicare, probably to encourage hospitals to serve Medicaid patients.

The same price disparity exists in prescription drug reimbursements. It is unbelievable that we have three government programs (Medicare Part D, Medicaid, and Veterans' Affairs) for prescriptions with a different cost structure for each program. You could also count the Defense Department as a purchaser of drugs for hospitals, infirmary and field operations, potentially creating a fourth level of pricing for the same drug. Is this rational?

When I asked hospital administrators what was the worst problem facing hospitals, the response was uniform: bad debt from uninsured middle class patients, the lack of the right mix of medical specialists on the hospital staff, and the lack of family practitioners who act as diagnosticians, or gatekeepers, and funnel patients into the system.

The bad debt problem is a direct result of the horrific cost of hospital services to the uninsured. Ultimately, the uninsured person who pays the full amount billed is subsidizing not only the "insured" patients, for whom the hospital will be paid only a portion of the total bill by the insurers, but also the bad debt resulting from the uninsured who do not pay. Who is this person who foots the bill for those that are insured, over 65, or very poor? Occasionally, it is the uninsured wealthy, but more often it is a person earning decent hourly wages but who still cannot afford health insurance. This entire situation can cause unbelievable financial hardship or bankruptcy, even for a non-lifethreatening illness or injury; that's not to mention the mental stress. Medical debt is the leading cause of bankruptcy in the U.S. The system is unjust, shameful and punitive.

Again, I can turn to my own life for anecdotal illustration. After undergoing many surgeries to repair the damage from my screwed-up cancer surgery, the hospital bills totaled more than $500,000. For most of the uninsured population (we are not talking about the wealthy here), that amount would almost certainly be impossible to pay, or would result in some form of bankruptcy. As it is, even with insurance and the reduced rate at which they approve the charges, a 20 percent co-pay in my case would have been substantial. How many of us have that money just laying around? Even the insured are at risk of bankruptcy or major financial hardship.

A substantial problem for the hospital industry is the fact that hospitals are mandated by law to treat patients regardless of ability to pay. They are forced to accept reimbursements from insurers that are less than the cost of the treatment, and to limit the amount of treatment and length of stay based on the insurance coverage. The pressure to move patients out the door often results in patients discharged while still in need of care, which can result in worsening of the problem, or, in the worst-case scenario, death. Malpractice lawsuits sometimes follow, causing catastrophic losses to the hospital and the insurer. The next domino in the chain is enormous malpractice insurance premiums for doctors and hospitals. This, in turn, causes hospital fees to rise to such a degree that the average patient is at a loss to understand why a simple pain reliever should cost $100.

Insurers point their fingers at the malpractice attorneys for perceived frivolous suits; the attorneys point to hospitals for improper care; the hospitals point to insurers for limiting coverage, and the problem of uninsured who cannot pay for their mandated treatment. Everyone is unhappy.

THE DOCTOR MACHINE

In 2005 there were an estimated 900,000 physicians in the United States practicing in 39 specialties, according to the American Medical Association (AMA). The top five specialties by number of practitioners are:

	1990	2005
Internal Medicine	98,000	154,000
Family Practice	49,000	82,000
Obstetrics/Gynecology	34,000	42,000
Pediatrics	42,000	67,000
Psychiatry	35,000	40,000

The lowest five are:

	1990	2005
Public Health	Not listed	1,500
General Preventive Medicine	Not listed	2,000
Forensic Pathology	Not listed	660
Aerospace Medicine	Not listed	500
Medical Genetics	Not listed	500

The rankings appear to be affected by two factors. The first is the natural desire of a person to pursue a field he is more comfortable with given his own talents and interests. The second is the area of medical service that will allow the doctor to pay off the more than $200,000 in debt accumulated in obtaining a medical degree and license, and the ability to achieve upper-class status.

The ratio of doctors of medicine to U.S. population is about 900,000 to 300,000,000, or one doctor for every 310 residents.

Primary doctors are either general practitioners or internal medicine specialists. These two physician groupings account for 210,000 primary care doctors, or a ratio of about one to 1,500 residents. Population density skews these numbers, with more doctors per capita in less populated areas, and fewer doctors per capita in densely populated areas. The income potential is also lower in rural areas, with fewer patients per doctor.

Health statistics are broken down into categories of population density only by states. This does not tell the whole picture, because health statistics can vary greatly between rural areas and more densely populated areas within each state, which are not accounted for in statewide statistics.

Doctors have been present and accounted for in my life. A doctor came to my parents' house to assist my mother in birthing me.

A doctor removed my tonsils in a small hospital. A doctor helped alleviate my pain when my back was broken playing high school football. A doctor tried to reduce my headaches when I was living as a monk studying to be a priest. A doctor misdiagnosed my stomachache and I spent a week in a hospital with acute appendix peritonitis while I was working and uninsured, saving my money for college. Goodbye savings!

Doctors were my neighbors and my boon companions when I was a Marine officer living in bachelor officer quarters. Those same companions – and the nurses in the military hospital – made sport of me when I was circumcised.

A doctor was walking next to the gurney with my wife aboard it on her way to a C-section and he asked how I, as a then-state senator, was going to vote on a bill near and dear to the AMA. Doctors were present when a car accident provided me with a concussion, broken collarbone and ribs. A poker-playing orthopedic doctor surgically relieved the gross pain in my back. A doctor popped me into intensive care with acute pneumonia and diagnosed sleep apnea during my stay. A doctor took my uvula and trimmed the interior fat of my mouth and throat and cut some of my tongue away, while blessing me with a tracheotomy for a few months.

Doctor after doctor tried to straighten out my crushed wrist from a fall on slippery ice; the third doctor finally got it right with a Hoffman device (which looks and functions like a tinker toy).

Doctors were good business partners and golf-club buddies, and it was doctors' skills in repeated knee surgeries that kept me on the course.

A cancer doctor found me with prostate cancer, the treatment of which resulted in the other problems described earlier. A lot of doctors looked at my case at many famous hospitals, but couldn't put Humpty Dumpty back together again—at least right away. Eventually, a team of doctors at Harper Hospital in Detroit succeeded after many hyperbaric treatments.

A doctor once asked me how I made it to his office on my feet, since my oxygen level was about 65 and should have been between 92 and 98. The doctor immediately put me in a wheel chair and pushed me to the intensive care unit of the hospital next door. Doctors made a difficult diagnosis of primary pulmonary arterial hypertension; during that hospital stay, another observant doctor noticed a previously undiscovered neuropathy in my legs.

I would like to come right out and say it: Thank God for doctors, hospitals, and their caring staffs.

PROPOSED SOLUTIONS

The U.S. must become a nation that looks to the health of its citizens. In order to achieve a healthy society, we must first become a nation of preventative medicine. The U.S. presumes to be a religious nation. Every religion historically has taught its followers to preserve their bodies by exercise and specific diets. Our nation is obese. Some doctors claim that fat is the home for cancerous cells and fat is the harbinger of heart and muscle problems. Others claim that the unnatural processed foods we ingest lead to myriad problems.

The first priority must be on preventive medicine—diet, exercise, clean air and healthy lifestyles, including the appropriate amount of rest.

Every municipality and school system in the U.S. has recreational facilities that were capital intensive to build; yet many remain underutilized. The U.S. needs more organized fitness programs, by age and capability, with qualified instructors. The federal and state government should either fund fitness programs or provide vouchers to be used at public or private facilities, like the YMCA or YWCA.

Doctors must receive more training in nutrition and physical fitness, and more doctors should be prescribing the same. Patients should be able to have the cost of a fitness and nutrition program reimbursed by our government or their private insurers.

United States companies cannot compete in the rest of the world, when we must add the $5,000-$12,000 health care cost per employee to the bottom line costs of doing business. The U.S. stands alone among major economic nations in its failure to provide universal health care. The federal government must coordinate with each state to develop a system that provides a base minimum health insurance for families, based on the particular needs of each state, and thus remove health insurance from the cost of doing business. Every U.S. resident and visitors to the U.S. should be treated to the best care possible, at minimal or no cost.

The U.S. must devise a system of uniform reimbursement rates for medical services. The governor of each state should appoint a board made up of representatives from hospitals, the health insurance industry, Medicare, Medicaid and the public to develop the system. Thus, the uninsured and the insured, either privately or by government program, would be expected to pay the same amount. The result would reduce the charges to the uninsured, as well as the amount care providers must absorb due to bad debt.

Families that choose, or are forced by financial circumstances, to care for an elderly parent should receive the same reimbursement as a nursing facility would from Medicare program. It may require a slightly greater stipend, because a normal household would not have the economics of scale that a nursing home could achieve.

The costs of educating and perfecting our doctors has escalated, causing a massive amount of debt for newly licensed physicians. The U.S. should institute a program of forgiveness of medical school debt for doctors who choose either less-populated areas or lower income-producing specialties.

The drug industry must be faced head on. Too many of the drugs tested by the Federal Drug Administration have been tested by shills for the drug producer; some are only marginally (three percent) more effective than the placebo they are tested against. Is it a wonder that the FDA is held in such low esteem? A new prescription-drug evaluation system is needed.

This new evaluation system must include speeding up the process from application to market approval. For instance, could the phase one, two and three of the clinical trials somewhat overlap?

Health problems should be prioritized by the number of people affected and the impact on those affected, taking into account cost of care, life expectancy, etc. The concept I propose would allocate funds for research according to these priorities.

In order to achieve proper funding for this research, all tax-free charitable trusts would be subject by law (regardless of their stated purposes) to a tax of 15 percent of their assets. There are about 72,000 charitable trusts; this would generate substantial funding, especially if matching federal funding is available.

These funds could be allocated to the drugs waiting for FDA approval. The FDA says there are about 200 cancer drugs waiting to be tested.

The World Almanac and Book of Facts lists 94 associations, such as the American Cancer Society, the American Heart Association, the Pulmonary Association etc., that are dedicated to finding cures and supporting patients of various medical conditions. A percentage of assets of other (non-medical) non-profits should, for a set period of time, be detoured to the resolution of our health problems by providing funds, management and volunteers to solving the problems of cancer, heart disease, diabetes etc.

Residents of the U.S. and of the world deserve drugs, treatments and cures that are reliable and effective. Our nation should not rest until we have provided ourselves and the rest of the world with cures, controls and medications that work effectively, not just marginally.

Part IV:
A GOVERNMENT FOR HALF THE PEOPLE?

"Politics ought to be the part-time profession of every citizen who would protect the rights and privileges of free people and who would preserve what is good and fruitful in our national heritage."
—*Dwight D. Eisenhower*

"The whole art of politics consists in directing rationally the irrationalities of men."
—*Reinhold Niebuhr*

"Your representative owes you, not his industry only, but his judgment; and he betrays, instead of serving you, if he sacrifices it to your opinion."
—*Edmund Burke*

One of the great hallmarks of American society is the fascinating variety of its people. We boast about our diversity in religious, social and political thought, ethnicity, interests, abilities and hobbies. We have traditionally celebrated this diversity hand in hand with the philosophy of individual freedom that our country was founded on. This freedom is reflected in our desire to be left alone, to enjoy the fruits of our labor without burdensome taxes or tyrannical government.

However, these two characteristics that define us as a society—freedom and diversity — create a dichotomy that is not easily resolved. Our diversity naturally divides us (officially or unofficially) into mini-constituencies or interest groups. Some examples are labor organizations, rifle clubs, medical research and support groups, etc. There are also constituencies that rely on government entitlements for day-to-day living. Each group has a particular set of needs and problems, and each expects the government to address or correct those needs and problems in some way, through funding or legislation. Consequently, we state a desire for a smaller government that will leave us alone, and at the same time expect it to swoop in like a superhero to solve our problems, be they big or small.

This contradiction creates unrealistic expectations and ultimately leads to disappointment in our government. It is doing too much, while simultaneously doing too little. The dichotomy manifests itself in an attitude toward government that sounds something like, "You need to reduce the size of government, cut the budget and lower my taxes—as long as you don't eliminate MY benefits!"

Americans must realize that they cannot have it both ways. If government is to be a problem solver, then we must accept the taxes, legislation and government programs that are necessary to make it happen. And in 2010, we have many problems to be solved. We live in a society that clings to a Constitution that served an aristocratic and agrarian constituency. The middle class is disappearing, the number of families that live in poverty is growing, millions have lost their jobs or homes, and bankers are playing Monopoly with worthless equities.

We need to get real! With so much at stake, the American people must get involved in creating a better future for the United States.

One of my favorite comic strips was called "Pogo;" it was created by Walt Kelly, and ran from 1948 to 1975, poking fun at political situations. One particular strip featured a conversation between two characters. Pogo was asked the question: What is more important—the financial world or the political world? Without hesitation, Pogo answered the political world. His friend probed further: Is it the money and expense accounts? Is it the perks, like being invited to all the best events? Is it the frills? The honor? To all of these Pogo responded "no." Finally the exasperated questioner asked: Is it the power? Pogo's face lit up with an emphatic "Ahh, that's the one!"

Thousands of people have a lot of money; hundreds of people have power. Only a handful have both money and power.

The average elected office-holder may have paid for his initial election with some of his own savings, borrowed funds, and money from his family, friends and supporters. He may also have received funds from endorsements or from his political party.

The few people with vast wealth and power can afford to fund their own election, and as office-holders have political power. These people are extremely scarce—and scary; they operate in two worlds, and can apply pressure in each. They include people like Michael Bloomberg of New York, and Arnold Schwarzenegger of California and the Kennedys of Massachusetts.

A wealthy individual donor may lock up the legislative votes of some office holders by contributing heavily to their campaigns. This is more prevalent with those newly elected to office. Elected officials in their first term, unless unusually savvy, have difficulty accomplishing much, rendering the benefactor's contributions futile. In subsequent terms of office, officials still receive individual contributions, although some put more stock in the latest public-opinion polls. Perhaps more importantly, too many office-holders dance to the tune of lobbyists.

So who ends up influencing the U.S. Senate and House of Representatives? Is it the elected officials, or is it their donors, their staffers, the lobbyists, various departmental bureaucrats, or the media? After election, members of Congress spend a disproportionate amount of time raising money for their re-election campaigns—the larger the war chest, the bigger deterrent to potential opponents.

In an article in the August 9, 2010 issue of *New Yorker* magazine, entitled "The Empty Chamber," author George Packer paints a sad scene of Congress. He writes about members relying on staffers and leaders for advice on how to vote on issues that were not considered in committees on which the members serve. Members in both houses spend Tuesday through Thursday each week in Committees, often away from public view.

The article also talks about Sen. Jeff Merkley (D-Ore.), who said that although the Senate is often referred to as "that great deliberative body," he has witnessed in his freshman term only one debate on the floor of the chamber between a Democrat and a Republican. He is quoted as saying it was a great debate; the only problem was that no one else was in the chamber to witness it.

CITIZEN PARTICIPATION

Since I was 12 years old, I have been volunteering for political campaigns and have served at every level, including campaign chairperson. The candidates I have worked for have ranged from school board members, city council members and mayors, state representatives and state senators, judges, governors, U.S. congressmen, U.S. senators, and U.S. presidents. I was the Michigan Co-Finance Chairperson for Bobby Kennedy's ill-fated run for president in 1968. Of the 20 campaigns where I was deeply involved, 14 of my candidates were elected and six were not.

There was a time in the 1920s, '30s and '40s when every household talked about politics (as they still do in Canada). People were involved in and belonged to local political clubs. Today, many political clubs represent either the Republican view (i.e. Chamber of Commerce) or the Democrat view (i.e. unions), restricting any discussion on matters not germane to their main purpose.

Many people do not like to talk politics outside their families and circles of friends who agree with them. In traditional debate, the illumination of the subject matter and the education involved is just as important as getting the better of your opponent. Has America lost its ability to discuss, debate and disagree? Perhaps we just want to avoid all arguments.

In 2004, 122 million votes were cast for president of the United States. In that same year, there were 229 million citizens over 18 years of age and eligible to vote. Why did 47 percent of eligible voters choose not to vote? Throughout the United States, even fewer people typically vote in state and local elections.

In 2008, 131,313,820 citizens voted in the presidential election, 58 percent of the approximately 225,499,000 eligible voters. In this election, more than 94 million voters (42 percent) did not vote. Voter turnout was higher than in 2004, but overall still a sad commentary.

In both elections the real suffering took place in the state and local elections. In many races in the U.S., candidates were elected to office by a minority of those eligible to vote. Why do people fail to uphold their civic responsibility? The common responses are: 1) "My vote doesn't make a difference." 2) "They're going to do what they want to anyway." 3) "They're all crooks!" 4) "They want to serve their own self-interest—they want the money, pension and perks." 5) "They're all lawyers!"

This is a severe problem, and the result is that we no longer act as a democratic republic. U.S. members of the House of Representatives often change districts every 10 years, after each U.S. census and its concomitant reapportionment. At one time, congressmen and state representatives represented a certain geographic area, with citizens who possessed a majority view on life and government. Both this majority and its counterpoint minority were vocal in their beliefs. This forced their elected representatives to pay close attention and vote accordingly.

In 1960, the Supreme Court ruled on fair apportionment—one

man, one vote. Thus, in 1964, districts were apportioned to almost equal population. In 1964, with a population of 180 million, a U.S. House of Representatives district represented an average of 418,000 residents. In 2010, it is projected there will be approximately 310 million residents in the country, and each House district will have about 713,000 residents.

According to Tom Woods in his 2010 book *Nullification*, when our Constitution was written in 1787 there were three million people in the U.S. and there were 100 members of Congress, for a ratio of one to 30,000. If we were to maintain that ratio today, we would have more than 10,000 members in the House of Representatives.

Perhaps it's time to review the ratio of representatives per capita, to obtain a government more responsive to the electorate. This would involve creating smaller districts and regional levels of government, making it more accountable to its electorate.

Now enter the vile, seditious gerrymanders. Gerrymandering is the process of manipulating districts to ensure an outcome favorable to incumbents and their colleagues. With gerrymandering came the beginning of real political downfall. Election districts on a national and state level are arranged, however crookedly and convolutedly, to preserve the balance of Republicans and Democrats that existed before the census in that particular state. Who benefits? The incumbents. Perhaps the major parties experience some gain in districts that change demographically. But the American people and their desires? Fat chance.

Also, local political clubs have suffered because of the geographic patchwork of districts. Subsequently, candidates for office have little familiarity or credibility with constituents because they lack a social background with other local party members.

The powers preserved for the states by the Tenth Amendment to our Constitution have been slowly emasculated by the federal government. The issue of "States' Rights" carries the misperception as being opposed to equal civil rights, as represented by Gov. George Wallace in the 1960s. What it really does is allow the states in their individual wisdom to deal with their unique needs and the nature of their particular constituency. The federal government has eroded the rights and powers of the states with regard to education, police powers, transportation, food regulation, agriculture—the list of issues goes on and on.

The U.S. Senate, whose original purpose was to act as a deliberative chamber, now acts as another House of Representatives. Senators are elected to terms of six years. This long-term provision enables Senators to take national (best for the country) and state views, not what is best for a particular district in the senator's state. The senate should, in light of its totally parochial vision, perhaps be eliminated.

In 2010, the U.S. Supreme Court ruled that private and public corporations, including labor unions, may spend money to elect or defeat a candidate, somehow claiming a First Amendment right for the corporations akin to that of an individual person. Previous courts and domestic scholars have attributed the rights enumerated in the first amendment to individual people or persons, i.e. "natural persons," not "artificial persons", such as corporations or associations. Unless controlled by legislation, big money will totally rule U.S. elections.

The current U.S. senators receive enormous contributions from the 25,000 lobbyists circling Washington D.C. like buzzards. Strangely enough, some senators vote with their conscience; but many vote according to lobbyist influence, longevity (re-election), perks and party wishes.

During the 2008 trillion-dollar Wall Street bailout, with Treasury Secretary Hank Paulsen and Federal Reserve Chairman Ben Bernanke leading the charge, I called an old acquaintance and political friend, Sen. Carl Levin (D) of Michigan. His staffer opined that the senator was busy, but there was nothing he could do about the legislation anyway—it was a done deal. I found the same situation as I called the offices of other Michigan legislators: Rep. Sander Levin (D), Rep. Candice Miller (R), and Rep. John Conyers (D)—I could only speak with their staffers. The responses were all the same; they followed the Bush administration's lead—the bailout was absolutely necessary, there was no other option. Finally, an old buddy, Rep. John Dingell (D), took my call, as graciously as ever. We talked for a long time, and John said "Eddie, I agree with your thoughts, but we have no choice." I was disappointed that Congress voted favorably on the bailout, but the members did it because they were told the banking system would fail if the bailout was not passed, causing another Great Depression.

Of particular interest was the situation with American International Group, Inc. (AIG). Little did I, a dumb cluck from East China, Michigan, understand that AIG would directly affect not only the invested pension funds of millions of government employees, but also every credit-granting entity in the U.S. As to the latter, assume that the fictional Roger E. Craig Department Stores (REC) decides it is tired of paying fees to the issuer of a customer's credit card. REC makes the decision to issue its own store credit card, but in doing so it is taking on some extensive risks. Now, along comes a company like AIG (or "Ain't I Good"), which offers to insure the risk.

This is exactly what happened with AIG. It had assumed too much risk through issuers of credit, and many of AIG's investments went sour, as well as those of many major banks. Toward the end of 2008, AIG panicked, causing a domino effect of panic throughout the credit industry. Secretary Paulsen called for a bailout of the banks, but barely mentioned AIG. The banks got TARP (Troubled Asset Relief Program) bailout money, but in the final analysis, AIG got the most money, even though it wasn't initially identified as a major failure. AIG was able to use the TARP money to pay its obligations to banks and credit issuers, including department stores. The banks soon claimed to be solvent again, and most paid back the TARP loan. And AIG keeps doing business with our money, but is still financially weak. Kick the money changers out of the temple!

THE CENTRIST PARTY SYSTEM

In the 2004 presidential race, the two major political parties garnered slightly more than 99 percent of the vote. That percentage went down slightly in 2008. There are about 15 different "third parties," most of which are on the ballot in only a few states. Taken together with write-in candidates, their parties typically receive a very small percentage (one percent) of the vote.

Americans speak about diversity when dealing with race, origin and sex, but not when it comes to political parties. How could the two candidates for president in 2004 be from the same school, same fraternity, the same club memberships, yet belong to opposing political camps? In 2009, the newly elected President Obama appointed cabinet members from the same businesses and institutions as his Republican predecessor.

In reality, there are two separate forces within each of our two major parties. The Republicans have conservatives and moderates, and the Democrats have liberals and moderates. At the same time, fifty percent of our citizens are without a known philosophical or political ideology. Without political beliefs, the citizens are more easily swayed by any demagogue that comes along. Are we leaving ourselves open to a revolution—peaceful or otherwise? And, if so, how do we correct this?

ELECTED OFFICE-HOLDERS

The governance of the United States at almost every level is by elected officials who must always take into consideration how they obtained their office. Many school boards are populated with the spouses of teachers and administrators, voting on matters affecting their spouses. School board elections are often scheduled to ensure a low, but favorable, turnout.

Mayors and city council members receive their campaign funds through contributions from the unions and small businesses they are to govern. Also, when elected, they have the toughest job in American politics because of easy access by their constituents.

The state legislatures are made up of both the best and the worst the political world has to offer. The worst of these are the politicians who pray they never have to take a position that is not supported by everyone. Content to draw salaries, expenses, free lunches, trips to sporting events and God only knows where else, these types of legislators are the constant "back-benchers." The best of the state legislators work hard from both an intellectual and time-commitment standpoint, don't hide from constituents, take the committee assignments, and go on to become governors and congressmen. They rise above the crowd as cream rises to the top.

MAJORITY PARTY STATUS

Whether it is the U.S. Capitol or the State Capitol, the most important item on a party's agenda is either staying in the majority or becoming the majority party in its chamber. One might believe this is to better foster the party's legislative agenda. Think again. Here is the real list of reasons:

1) To secure more attention and money from lobbyists and bureaucrats for the office-holders' re-election. The lobbyists and bureaucrats believe their largesse will be rewarded by attention and

potential action from majority party members. These politicos can return time and time again to the deep pockets of lobbyists, regaling them with the stupendous efforts they are putting forth to bring about the desired legislation or resolution, to reduce bureaucratic harassment, to secure a spot on a qualified bidder list, or some other perk in the lobbyists' interest. Furthermore, this scenario will continue, in a lucrative cycle for the legislators, until another clueless legislator (usually a first-termer) accidentally performs the desired deed and kills the golden egg of lobbyist money.

For example, when I was a freshman state senator, a bill to allow Sunday liquor sales had passed the state house; in the state senate, it was reported out of committee after several years and was placed on the table awaiting a majority vote. I was in favor of the bill, and moved to put it to a vote, where it passed. Thus ended the contributions from the liquor lobby as well as my relationship with the original sponsor, who had no intention of actually passing the bill but every intention of continually accepting the lobby contributions.

2) To chair one or more committees; the chairman of each committee is assigned a nice office, and allowed to appoint his own staff. The more important the committee, the bigger everything is—the office, the staff, the fundraising budget, the travel perks, etc.

3) To facilitate more exposure on T.V., radio, cable, newsprint than minority party members, because majority members can make things happen, right?

4) To gain more respect and quicker response from cabinet department personnel. This is very important in serving those bothersome voters.

5) To champion "banner issues," which are unique to each party and typically pander to the party base. An example of this is minimum-wage legislation, which is typically supported by Democrats and opposed by Republicans; another example is "right to work" legislation, which is typically supported by Republicans and opposed by Democrats.

The differences between the two major parties are illustrated by two anecdotes, involving committee hearings in both the House and the Senate.

On November 14, 2007, the House Subcommittee on Commerce Oversight, chaired by Democrat Bart Stupak of Michigan, held a hearing related to the use of carbon monoxide on meat to make it look red, thereby improving the appearance to the customer and thus increasing shelf life.

Appearing before the Commerce Oversight Subcommittee in the House were the presidents of Hormel and Agrica. The Democrats on the committee were concerned about doctored meat appearance (red color) used to extend its useful life to an unsuspecting public. Republicans said no complaints had been made to the companies, and the expiration date had been made more visible.

It appeared to me that the real, unstated issue was that the meat companies sought to increase shelf life and thereby reduce their discarded meat costs, and the meat providers i.e. cattle, hog, lamb and poultry farmers were losing sales to the meat companies in direct proportion to the extended shelf life.

Contributing to the problem was the fact that the various government agencies—the Food and Drug Administration and the Agriculture Department—were silent with respect to rules and regulations under the George W. Bush administration.

Congressman John Dingell (D-Mich.) cut to the tenderloin of the matter, stating that the problem might be with unscrupulous meat purveyors in discount meat operations, serving poor people, and the failure of the administrative agencies to set forth guidelines.

On the same day, another hearing was held in the Senate Finance Committee by Senator Max Baucus, a Democrat from Wyoming, relating to the estate tax. This hearing was extremely enlightening. It waged an almost classic discussion about the distribution of income. The hearing was held at the request of Senator Chuck Grassley, a Republican of Idaho, on behalf of a farmer constituent; the ultimate goal of the hearing and subsequent legislation was to eliminate the estate tax.

On one hand was Warren Buffet, who was in favor of the estate tax, and on the other hand were three who opposed the estate tax: a famous CPA and professor, a rancher from Nevada whose wife inherited their spread, and an Idaho farmer who was worried about his children and grandchildren who now worked in his multi-state agribusiness. (Curiously, two of the three grandchildren who "worked" for the company were going to college—an interesting tax dodge only available to family owned businesses.) The three were horribly outmatched by Warren Buffet.

The estate tax appears to impact between 9,000 and 12,000

families in the United States; they are the heirs of deceased individuals who created a business, employed people, caused economic multipliers, and in most cases, were a boon to the local community, donating to many charitable causes. The heirs who want to take over the business must pay this tax. This imposes a hardship on the heirs, who often borrow the money to pay the tax or must sell the company in order to pay it.

Buffet stated that for most children, tomorrow is not promised. The sons of football or baseball players do not inherit their fathers' team spots. Both the estate tax question and the meat-coloring issue are metaphors for the dilemma facing the free uncontrolled or unmanaged economy.

The hearings were held by two different congressional panels. Both discussions were considering relatively minor aspects of the economy. The two committees spent hours on minutiae, thus avoiding the real issues of the day. With regard to meat coloring, that issue should be handled by an administrative rule-making committee, representing the consumer, the food industry and a neutral federal district court referee. Of course, the committee would be subject to legislative and judicial oversight.

Small businesses that grow and develop into big or major businesses are the heartbeat of the U.S. economy. In the case of the estate tax, the government should provide for interest-free payments over a period of years, and if not paid by the end of that period, a forced sale of the company should take place, with the cumulative estate taxes paid from the sale.

LOBBYISTS AND BUREAUCRATS

When I was a state senator, I often wondered whether there was a difference between the private lobbyists seeking advantage for their clients, and bureaucrats attempting to increase the share of the budget for their favorite program.

Federal budget expenditures increased by $700 billion from 2000 to 2005; the Defense Department accounted for 28 percent of this increase. Medicare and Medicaid accounted for another 34 percent of the expenditure jump. Social Security payments jumped $120 billion, or 17 percent. The remaining 21 percent was spread amongst the other hungry departments with the help of their legislative liaison personnel (lobbyists).

The number of lobbyists registered in Washington D.C. is more than 24,000, and their numbers are more than replicated in the states. Thirty-seven of the 50 state legislatures meet every year, and the remaining 13 meet every other year. The State of Michigan has 2,500 registered lobbyists. Lobbyists attempt to change or kill legislation affecting their clients, to create new legislation, and to seek appropriations or grants for their clients. Lobbyists may act alone or in conjunction with other legislative agents—often from the same industry or similar organizations.

Often perceived as corrupters or twisters, good lobbyists or legislative agents can be a source of information or research for legislators seeking knowledge related to bills

Unelected bureaucrats survive from one administration to the next, but their numbers are small in comparison to Civil Service employees. It is the civil servants who run every department at every level of government, and unlike elected officials, they aren't subject to re-election; you can't throw the bums out.

In 1995, the employment rolls of federal, state and local government totaled 17 million. By 2004, the number of government civilian employees was 19.4 million. The Service Employees International Union grew from 960,000 members in 1995 to 1.6 million members in 2004, a 64 percent increase. The combined union affiliation of teachers in the National Education Association and the American Federation of Teachers reached 4 million in 2004, a 1.2 million member increase (43 percent) in the 10 years since 1995.

The combined three labor organizations of government employees, service workers and teachers represented more than 50 percent of the total union members in the U.S. in 2004. These unions have grown and enriched their members through increased salaries and benefits. Talk about a powerful lobby!

Teachers are unique in comparison with other union members because they are protected in many states by the tenure system as well as by their union agreements. As a result, teachers enjoy unusual job security and comfort, with little regard to job performance. In some districts, teachers' average salary and benefits taken together amount to more than $100,000 per year. The average person who enjoys two weeks of vacation per year works about 250 days per year. A teacher works fewer than 40 weeks, or 200 days, per year.

As teachers move into administrative positions, their salaries in those positions have been based on the pay of similar positions in other districts across the state, regardless of district size. This puts an undue burden on small districts and their taxpayers.

FUNNY MONEY

Consistently in U.S. politics, committees arise for a specific stated purpose, then promote secret agendas. Moreover, political parties often exceed individual states' spending rules through shifting funds from one state to another without reporting it.

Many are familiar with the ads run by 'Swift Boat Veterans for Truth' in the 2004 presidential election to discredit the military service of Democratic nominee John Kerry. The veterans quoted in the ad were identified, but individual donors to the organization remained unidentified. According to a September 26, 2010 article in the *New York Times* entitled "Secret, Tax-Exempt Dollars Fund Political Fights," an organization called Americans for Job Security spent $1.6 million in Alaska in 2006 pushing a referendum to restrict mining for gold and copper. Americans for Job Security is a 501 (c)(6) organization, which does not have to report its source of income, according to the article. In Michigan, the same organization ran ads against the 2010 Democratic nominee for governor. A provision of the 501(c)(6) is that the members of and donors to the organization do not need to be disclosed. However, it is a criminal violation of the Charitable Trust Act to use tax-exempt funds for political purposes.

PROPOSED SOLUTIONS

Unions for government employees pose a particular problem in America. They vote as citizens, and then they negotiate for benefits with those they elected, which presents a conflict of interest. This is sometimes resolved by the appointment of arbitrators, who generally rule in favor of the employees. Currently, arbitrators are chosen in part by the two parties represented. A better system would involve random selection of arbitrators by drawing.

Teachers must choose between the state tenure system and their union protections. Having two different "life-support" systems puts teachers in a never-lose situation, which is bad for students, parents, school districts and, ultimately, the nation. Also, administrative pay within school districts should be based on district size and student population rather than being standardized across the state.

Our two major political parties have made it extremely difficult to start a new (third) party; most, except those headed by well-known individuals like George Wallace, Ralph Nader or Ross Perot, give up because of the horrendous requirements to place its candidates on ballots. The requirements are different in each state. These requirements to place third-party and independent candidates on ballots should be reasonable, to level the playing field with the Democrat and Republican parties that were grandfathered in when the regulations were written.

In order to facilitate more participation, elections should be held on a National Election Day, a state and federal holiday; it would be best to make it a Wednesday. A Friday or Monday date would run contrary to the purpose because some people would view it as a minivacation and head for the hills and lakes.

Time limitations should be imposed for campaigns for the president and vice-president. Other countries have proven that time limitations are effective.

Spending limitations need to be enacted and the limit per candidate must include all sources of funding for a candidate, including:

- The candidate's personal fundraising expenditures
- The political party expenditures on behalf of a candidate
  (including that which hides behind "independent"
  organizations such as Americans for Job Security)
- All out-of-state expenditures for a candidate
- All corporate and union expenditures for a candidate

Additionally, tax-exempt organizations should not be allowed to use funds for political purposes, and other independent organizations should be required to disclose individual or corporate donors of funds used for political purposes.

Further, all licensed television, radio and cable networks and stations must provide a certain number of free prime-time minutes to each candidate for president or candidates for other major offices within the limited campaign time. This would replace the paid advertising time purchased with campaign funds. The same should happen in every state for state candidates.

Term limits should be removed in order for legislators, governors and even presidents to grow in their positions, increasing their knowledge and ability to serve. The clout of lobbyists and bureaucrats can be reduced by eliminating the need of newly elected officials to rely on them.

Political claims of office-holders must be made to be 100 percent truthful—no claiming responsibility for every good thing that happens during their terms and eschewing every bad thing in their political arena. Office-holders' newsletters regarding their accomplishments should not be funded by the state or federal government within 90 days of an election; during this time, the funding should come from campaigns. Some media outlets specialize in ferreting out the truth of political claims. These are the sources that should be relied on by the public.

Restrictions should be set on travel and entertainment paid for by both public and private lobbyists and liaisons.

Lobbyists and bureaucrats should have limited access to officeholders and their staffs. Everyone is free to attend public hearings. Meetings with legislators should be at the discretion of the legislator. Staff members should report all contacts with legislative agents and government representatives.

Spending by lobbyists and civil liaisons on office-holders should be restricted.

Legislative districts should not only have similar populations; they should be based on a standard grid, not randomly drawn for political gain, and be responsive to the population of the district. We are a democracy.

Defeated, term-limited or retired legislators should be barred from lobbying for private or public entities and may not run for a seat in another chamber of the state or nation until one full subsequent term of that body has expired.

Sitting judges should not be allowed to endorse candidates.

Elected office is a public service. I hate the "I'm sacrificing, now pay me handsomely" attitude.

According to an NBC and *Wall Street Journal* poll released on September 26, 2010, 25 percent of those surveyed looked favorably on the

Tea Party movement, which is advocating major changes in our government. Perhaps a call for national and/or state constitutional conventions is necessary. If we do not change the *modus operandi* of our current political system peacefully, change will come violently.

Part V:
LET THE EAGLE SOAR

"Some people see things as they are and say why. I dream things that never were and say why not?"
    —*George Bernard Shaw*

The most difficult thing to accomplish in any society is change. Whether it is in business, education, unions or government, when someone says "Let's change the way we do things," people become alarmed. In this chapter, the changes I describe may be viewed as radical—because they are. However, unconventional proposals are not necessarily bad ideas. What I've proposed here is where I would like to see our nation end up, but I realize that not all the changes can be made in one stroke. A gradual implementation must be utilized.

UNIVERSAL NATIONAL SERVICE CORPS

A mandatory national training program should be in place for all residents above the age of seventeen. The goals of this paid training experience would be to expose young citizens (corps members) to the opportunities that exist in our society, to provide hands-on education, and to create a certain standard of citizenship. During the entire training and service program, participants would be housed together in government-provided quarters. There would be three main components that would be undertaken consecutively.

1) Your Healthy Body: All participants would learn how to achieve and maintain good health. This would include physical fitness for all, including customized programs for those physically challenged or handicapped; there would also be emphasis on nutrition and food variety, lifestyle, sports, dental and physical hygiene. This would create a blueprint not only for healthy Americans, but also a healthy America. The duration of this component would be one to two months.

2) Military Service: All individuals would participate in fitness training (similar to military basic training) to achieve their maximum

physical potential. This would include those physically challenged or handicapped. Young people are currently often denied the opportunity for military service because of conditions such as high blood pressure, asthma, diabetes or other common ailments. Rather than turn them away, this program would give those individuals the opportunity to manage their health conditions as part of their military training. This portion of the training would last four to six weeks.

In the next phase, corps members would learn to use current firearms, participate in firing-range programs and become familiar with all types of military equipment. They would receive some education in military strategy and intelligence, and participate in both offensive and defensive tactics in differing situations. This phase would last four months, during the final six weeks of which trainees would be assigned normal military billets or duties, according to their physical and/or mental capabilities. They would perform these duties with regular service personnel.

During some portion of this training, all individuals would be taught civilized manners in all aspects of life: seating, table manners, pedestrian walking, auto driving and general good behavior that provides peace in the valley. My own military training taught me, among other things, that if I was walking eastward and an individual was walking toward me westward, we both should move to the right so we should avoid running into each other. In a truly perfect world, this type of teaching should be done by parents, but it is not happening that way.

3) Civilian Service. This 12-month period would provide an opportunity for young people to explore various types of careers and community or government services. This would provide a benefit to the trainees, and also to the communities and businesses that participate in the training.

The first portion of the training program would explore career paths and knowledge of both private and public careers and service. It should explain both the large business and the niche spin-off little companies, as well as all aspects of owning your own business. The same would be true of all levels of government operations. This might take three months, with two months devoted to business and one month devoted to government, or vice versa.

The second phase or portion would be devoted to mini working internships, either in business or government sectors, for a nine-month period. This program would be structured so that trainees receive three three-month assignments, based on the trainee's expressed interest and aptitude.

By way of example, if a corps member expressed an interest in manufacturing, he might be assigned first to a small shop for three months, then to a medium-sized shop or factory and finally to a large factory. If a corps member wanted to become a media person, he would be assigned first to a newspaper or news website, then to a TV or cable station, then to a P.R. or advertising firm. Or if a corps member was interested in medicine perhaps a program would include three months at a pharmacy, three months in a doctor's office and three months in a hospital. Trainees may also choose from assignments in more than one discipline or category.

4) Beginning a Career Path. At this point, the corps member will have been instructed on a clean, healthy lifestyle; introduced to other people, food, and lifestyles; given military offensive and defensive training; presented with education on business and government; and experienced either business or government employment in several real-life situations.

In a retreat-like environment, the corps member would examine his experiences, and begin to think about life and career objectives and make some tentative decisions. He may a) go immediately to work; b) attend a community college to further explore life options and goals; c) attend a trade school; d) attend a college or university.

Those who choose trade school, community college or university would receive a stipend from Uncle Sam for modest room and food. The tuition would be subsidized in two ways:

The student would provide labor to the university or college in exchange for a portion of the tuition. In my perfect world, the school would begin replacing a portion of non-faculty employees with students. Universities should operate as cities unto themselves. This would be reminiscent of a monastery, where all work is performed by the monks, from farming, construction and maintenance to printing, library work, etc. This would apply to undergraduate and graduate-level schools, including legal, medical, etc. The remainder of the tuition should be paid for by the state the school resides in.

In order for the system to work, and for students to complete their education in two to four years, students should take no fewer than seventeen credits per semester, with only a slight summer break.

If we say that children are our future, then let us prepare all of them with two educations. The first and primary education is the value of life, knowledge for its own sake, and personal and interpersonal relationships and creating a better society. The second is the acquiring of knowledge for a skill or for employment.

An often heard lament is "I have a great education, but I cannot get a job." Liberal arts and business colleges can provide a wonderful general education experience. Specialized schools for engineering, medical and scientific fields, law, and education teach students who are seeking a narrow field of training.

James Madison, our fourth president, said "Knowledge will forever govern ignorance: and a people who mean to be their own governors, must arm themselves with the power knowledge gives."

Free education was traditionally an integral part of British and European culture and, more recently (after the fall of the dynasties), has propelled China and Japan to economic greatness. Only recently, burdened by the current economic depression and requirements of the European Union, have European resident students had to pay modest tuitions in their own country (compared to the U.S.). Non-resident students pay dearly for a European education.

INFORMATION SUPERHIGHWAY

Whether you are watching television, listening to radio, reading a newspaper, texting, Twittering or in conversation with a friend, the Internet is the word and the world. Mainstream media and businesses make the mistaken assumption that everyone has Internet access. Yet, as a nation, we are not up to speed. The *U.S. Census Bureau Current Population Survey* reported the following in 2009:

Number of Households	129,922,000
Number of Households with Computers	119,296,000
Number of Households Without Computers	10,622,000
Number of Households With Internet Access	81,957,000
Number of Households Without Internet Access	47,968,000

Tom Friedman, in his bestseller *The World Is Flat*, laid out a new world based on the use of the Internet. A flat world is the world of the Corporations Without Borders. It is created to eliminate any burdens of manufacturing, marketing and selling a product. The "Same-ing of America" is being followed by the "Same-ing of Europe." The flattening of Europe (through the formation of the European Union) will transform wonderfully individualized, unique countries into a standardized market for the Corporations Without Borders. This standardization of the world marketplace will facilitate the eventual elimination of most traditional communication methods in favor of the Internet for the use of advertising and marketing.

I get sick conjuring up the "sameness" of every place. A flat world is not my world.

On the other hand, there is a crying need to bring our country into the new world of information technology. The nearly 11 million households without computers or 37 million with computers and no Internet access scream for educational justice. One of those households may be the home of a potential Thomas Edison, Madame Curie or Washington Carver. It is criminal. The richest nation in the world denies access to knowledge to many of its residents based on poverty, illness or ignorance.

We must enable all our residents to access information. Bill Gates of Microsoft has nobly offered, through his foundation, to end malaria in Africa. Perhaps his foundation could provide computers to those who do not have them, and Internet access to those currently without access. In the process, through education on use, and uplifting more consumers through knowledge, Microsoft just might develop more customers. If Bill doesn't do it alone, it may be done in concert with Google and other computer companies. If not done through charitable foundations, the states must do it through their school systems.

UNEMPLOYMENT

It is not socialist to ask private businesses and investment capitalists to join the government in assuring that the unemployment rate does not fall below five percent nationally. Likewise, at the state level, the private sector and government should work in concert to achieve temporary unemployment rates less than seven percent. Programs such as giving tax incentives to businesses for hiring and retaining employees, or a public-works program should be developed to keep the unemployment numbers down.

We also must have a more descriptive definition of "unemployed." There are at least five levels of unemployment:

1) Individuals receiving unemployment benefits or private or union supplemental unemployment plans

2) Individuals temporarily unemployed for medical reasons

3) Individuals with disabilities that preclude employment

4) Individuals off the unemployment rolls, whose benefits have expired but are still seeking employment, or who have accepted part-time work but are still seeking full-time jobs

5) Individuals who have given up looking for work and are receiving welfare and Medicaid

PUTTING PEOPLE TO WORK

Many types of stimulus programs carry not only the immediate benefit of creating jobs, but also long-term or permanent benefits for society, economic and otherwise.

The very first economic stimulus program should be the placement of all utilities safely underground, away from land faults and other fissures. We have the capability to do that now. We do it in our downtowns and in much of our new construction. This should be a long-term program (from 20 to 50 years), which would create thousands of jobs.

In the immediate term, the economic problems caused by power outages will be reduced. These problems include: loss of productivity for closed businesses, and resultant increased product cost; cost to the utility company of the repairs, which is passed on to the consumer; and the cost of spoiled food.

The personal hardships due to power outages include: loss of heat or air conditioning in homes or offices, which is especially hard on senior citizens and families with young children; loss of elevator use; and reduced personal and home security due to crime and looting. Darkness is the enemy of all good people and the ally of the devil.

The economic generator of such a program would be multi-fold: the utility and construction workers and their families would enjoy some financial stability for the duration of the project. They, in turn, would spend money in their community, which would result in economic growth in many other sectors—retail, banking, services, legal, medical, education and so on.

The aesthetic benefits are also tangible. Imagine driving or looking out your home window without seeing telephone poles carrying a mishmash of wires for electricity, telephone and cable lines.

The cost of the program would be shared by the government and the utility companies, which would be permitted to float revenue bonds to pay for their share of the cost of construction. Until the bonds are paid off, the utility companies must absorb 50 percent of the bond payments, and only pass 50 percent of the cost to their consumers.

If, in the 21st century, we are to continue our movement toward a more perfect nation, the underground utility program should be high on our list.

TOWARD A MORE PERFECT
TRANSPORTATION SYSTEM

Our transportation system is critical and essential for our economy and our national defense, but it's currently a mess! We have an opportunity to create years of employment with economic growth. A more perfect coordination and utilization of our transportation system would greatly enhance our current movement of people, goods and services.

Consider the benefits of an updated system that provided more economic and timely delivery of people, goods and supplies, and with greater ease and comfort for our nation and our people. This would affect:

1) Long-term employment related to construction and maintenance of the system

2) People traveling to and from work and retail shopping areas

3) Small businesses in the movement of supplies both in and out

4) Retail prices and profits due to reduced costs

Our government has already heavily subsidized the airlines and airports. It has provided funds for Amtrak. However, after several inquiries to various subcommittees of the House Ways and Means Committee, I could not determine if any subsidies (other than tax considerations) exist for the shipping and the trucking industry. Why don't they exist?

A series of transportation business centers should be created, either by private business, government or in combination, to advise businesses on transportation solutions involving all means of transport (trucks, trains, ships and planes). This service would benefit the private sector the same way that travel agents advise and consolidate services for travelers.

Finally, the Jones Act regulating foreign- and U.S.-flag shipping and needs to be revised to reflect our current economic situation.

TRUCKING AND HIGHWAYS

In the U.S., trucking is essential to both our economy and our national defense. Yet Americans, especially in northern climes, suffer through road repair after road repair. What is the problem? Are the trucks overloaded? Are the roadbeds improperly built? Does the road design include programmed obsolescence in order to ensure continuing work for the road-builders? Are the road-builders and the Department of Transportation too friendly with each other, resulting in little accountability?

It is time to separate passenger highways and trucking highways. New trucking highways could be built specifically for heavy commercial loads; with proper bedding and construction of the roadway, potholes could be greatly reduced or eliminated. The roadbed should be built to withstand 110 percent of the heaviest load potential of the next generation of engines. The roadbeds should also include internal drainage and should chemically prohibit icing in winter states. Additionally, this construction should consist of all concrete. Asphalt contains oil residue from petroleum refining; avoiding its use would help reduce our dependence on oil products. Finally, these truck-only highways should include decent truck stop accommodations for drivers.

While costing more to build initially, these roads would need far less maintenance in the future, and would have a longer lifespan than the typical highway of today, saving money over time. The new truck highways could be paid for with tax-free state revenue bonds. The bonds would be retired using a mileage tax on trucks. Another approach would be for private companies to bid for the rights to build, manage and maintain the trucking highways, charging tolls or other usage fees.

Our existing passenger freeways should be rebuilt simultaneously and abreast with the new trucking highways. Construction should be to the same standards as the trucking highways, but designed for the vehicle weight of passenger or light commercial vehicles. This would ensure their longevity.

The program for both trucking and passenger highways might take 20 to 40 years, but what a great boost for economics in the construction and long-term cost savings. And imagine the enjoyment and convenience of travel for both passenger vehicles and trucks.

TRAINS

The U.S. is home to stupendous vistas, which could be viewed from passenger trains (if we still had them!). For most of the U.S., train travel has been fossilized for both commercial and passenger traffic. The newer rail systems on the East Coast, the West Coast and the corridor from New York to Washington D.C. should serve as a model for the rest of the country. Perhaps Warren Buffet's purchase of the Burlington, Northern, Santa Fe Railroad Company indicates that he knows something about the future of the railroad business, or that he will make something happen. This could be a harbinger of good things in the industry.

The U.S. should attempt to acquire (by gift, purchase or condemnation) all railroad tracks, their right-of-ways, spur tracks and train stations. The government should then contract with engineering and design firms to design replacement tracks for both commercial and passenger use that are able to respond to both types of traffic, providing a smooth floating ride. The tracks are the key to a pleasant passenger ride, as well as for secure boxcar transport.

The design would provide for all street crossings to be above grade (by bridge) or below grade (by tunnel), in order to eliminate railroad crossing on surface roads or highways.

The construction of the rail tracks, bridges and tunnels should follow a 20- to 50-year time schedule. The construction would again be financed by combined federal and state revenue bonds. The bonds would be retired by a use tax levied in cents per mile. As this program is gradually completed, the administration and ownership would be transferred to the state wherein the tracks lay. U.S. regional coordinators would provide necessary coordination in scheduling and to ensure track maintenance and safety.

The benefits of such a plan would be many: the design and construction phase would provide thousands of immediate jobs; as the program evolves, permanent employment would occur in maintenance and management of the rail system.

By eliminating crossings at grade level, trains would be able to move at greater speeds, thus increasing efficiency. It would also eliminate the danger of vehicle and pedestrian accidents and loss of lives. Furthermore, the differential between air travel and shipping versus the rail system would become much smaller, and in many cases might cost less, be more convenient and provide a more enjoyable experience.

Another common but less-publicized problem with railroad crossings would be eliminated: the loss of man hours caused by waiting for long, slow freight trains. Trains often exceed a state's time limitations on grade crossings. A train that causes a backup of 200 cars for 10 minutes (as they do at one crossing in Detroit) causes the loss of 33.3 man hours, not to mention the collective burning of the same number of gallons of gas. A police car at idle burns one gallon of gas per hour, according to a study conducted by the Ann Arbor, Michigan, Police Department.

A similar problem exists with drawbridges for boat traffic. In some areas a single, relatively small boat causes the bridge to rise, forcing up to a hundred cars to wait. Marinas and boat dockage should be limited to the main river or waterway, without any crossings that interfere with road traffic.

The ideas I have proposed will, of course, be dismissed by both liberals and conservatives who have locked-in points of view. The U.S. Constitution and its amendments are interpreted through the eyes of the beholder.

Everyone agrees we are a nation in trouble, almost devoid of humor and reasonable debate. The early United States created an environment that allowed persons (whether corporate—artificial—persons or real persons) to grow and fulfill their dreams. Today, our Congress is a muscle-bound entity, enslaved by its own rules and its constant electioneering. What may be proposed by a Democratic Congress in an earlier year is later killed by the same Democrats when brought forward by a Republican Congress, and vice versa. They are tigers without teeth, spinning tales without producing yarn, much less significant bi-partisan laws.

Patriotism, as our founders believed, is a nation of one people under God, all for one and one for all. But patriotism is not just about defending our country and waving our flag. Patriotism also means that we look to the effect of our actions on our fellow countrymen, and on future generations.

Corporations and businesses that replace U.S. labor with cheap foreign labor, and then bring the foreign product back to the U.S. to sell are not patriotic. Unions that demand more for their toil than their productivity justifies are not patriotic. Companies that engage in mergers and acquisitions that reduce competition and result in job losses are not patriotic.

Today, the United States is a great nation, but is it as great as it could or should be? We need a call to action, just as we were called to action at the beginning of World War II. The call should not be for Koreas, Vietnams, Iraqs or Afghanistans. The call is for the economic salvation of our country. Unless we undertake some drastic new direction, our flag will start to droop. Let's use our intellect and common sense to fulfill our potential for greatness and bring glory to our star-spangled banner.

APPENDIX A
FEDERAL INCOME VS. FEDERAL SPENDING
(by president's administrative budget)

The budget in the first year of each presidency is determined by the President of the previous year.

President	Year	Income (thousands)	Spending (thousands)	Deficit / Surplus (thousands)	
Kennedy (D)	1961	$94,388,000	$97,723,000	$-3,335,000	-3.5%
"	1962	$99,676,000	$106,821,000	$-7,146,000	-7.1%
"	1963	$106,560,000	$111,316,000	$-4,756,000	-4.4%
Johnson (D)	1964	$112,613,000	$118,528,000	$-5,915,000	-5.2%
"	1965	$116,817,000	$118,228,000	$-1,411,000	-1.2%
"	1966	$130,835,000	$134,562,000	$-3,698,000	-2.8%
"	1967	$148,822,000	$157,464,000	$-8,643,000	-5.8%
	1968	$152,973,000	$178,134,000	$-25,161,000	-16.4%
Nixon (R)	1969	$186,882,000	$183,640,000	$3,242,000	+1.7%
"	1970	$192,807,000	$195,649,000	$-2,842,000	-1.4%
"	1971	$187,139,000	$210,172,000	$-23,033,000	-12.3%
"	1972	$207,309,000	$230,681,000	$-23,373,000	-11.2%
"	1973	$230,799,000	$245,707,000	$-14,908,000	-6.4%
Ford (R)	1974	$263,224,000	$269,359,000	$-6,135,000	-2.3%

"	1975	$279,090,000	$332,332,000	$-53,242,000	-19.0%
"	1976	$298,060,000	$371,792,000	$-73,732,000	-24.0%
Carter (D)	1977	$355,559,000	$409,218,000	$-53,659,000	-15.1%
"	1978	$399,561,000	$458,746,000	$-59,185,000	-14.8%
"	1979	$463,302,000	$504,028,000	$-40,726,000	-8.8%
"	1980	$517,112,000	$590,941,000	$-73,830,000	-14.3%
Reagan (R)	1981	$599,272,000	$678,241,000	$-78,968,000	-13.1%
"	1982	$617,766,000	$745,743,000	$-127,977,000	-21.3%
"	1983	$600,562,000	$808,364,000	$-207,802,000	-34.6%
"	1984	$661,486,000	$851,853,000	$-185,367,000	-27.8%
"	1985	$734,088,000	$946,396,000	$-212,308,000	-28.9%
"	1986	$769,215,000	$990,430,000	$-221,215,000	-28.7%
"	1987	$854,353,000	$1,004,082,000	$-149,728,000	-17.5%
"	1988	$909,303,000	$1,064,455,000	$-155,152,000	-17.1%
G.H.W. Bush (R)	1989	$991,190,000	$1,143,646,000	$-152,456,000	-15.4%
"	1990	$1,031,969,000	$1,253,165,000	$-221,195,000	-21.4%
"	1991	$1,055,041,000	$1,324,369,000	$-269,320,000	-25.5%
"	1992	$1,091,279,000	$1,381,655,000	$-290,376,000	-26.6%
Clinton (D)	1993	$1,154,401,000	$1,409,489,000	$-255,087,000	-22.4%
"	1994	$1,258,627,000	$1,461,877,000	$203,250,000	-16.1%
"	1995	$1,351,830,000	$1,515,802,000	$-163,972,000	-12.1%
"	1996	$1,453,062,000	$1,560,535,000	$-107,473,000	-7.3%

"	1997	$1,579,292,000	$1,601,250,000	$-21,958,000	-1.3%
"	1998	$1,721,798,000	$1,652,585,000	69,213,000	+4.0%
"	1999	$1,827,454,000	$1,701,891,000	$125,563,000	+6.8%
"	2000	$2,025,218,000	$1,788,773,000	$236,445,000	+11.6%
G.W. Bush (R)	2001	$1,991,194,000	$1,863,770,000	$127,424,000	+6.3%
"	2002	$1,853,173,000	$2,010,970,000	$-157,797,000	-8.5%
"	2003	$1,782,342,000	$2,157,637,000	$-375,295,000	-21.0%
"	2004	$1,830,071,000	$2,292,215,000	$-415,144,000	-21.9%
"	2005	$2,153,859,000	$2,472,205,000	$-318,346,000	-14.5%
"	2006	$2,407,254,000	$2,655,435,000	$-248,181,000	-10.3%
"	2007	$2,540,096,000	$2,784,267,000	$-244,176,000	-9.6%
"	2008	$2,662,474,000	$2,901,861,000	$-239,387,000	-9.0%
Obama (D)	2009	$2,699,947,000	$3,091,340,000	$-391,393,000	-14.5%

Source: U.S. Office of Management and Budget

APPENDIX B
2009 WORLDWIDE CAR PRODUCTION STATISTICS

COUNTRY	CARS	COMMERCIAL VEHICLES	TOTAL
Argentina	380,067	132,857	512,924
Australia	188,158	39,125	227.283
Austria	56,620	15,714	72,334
Belgium	524,595	12,510	537,354
Brazil	2,576,628	605,989	3,182,617
Canada	822,267	668,365	1,490,632
China	10,383,831	3,407,163	13,790,994
Czech Republic	967,760	6,809	974,569
Egypt	60,249	32,090	92,339
Finland	10,907	64	10,971
France	1,819,462	228,196	2,047,658
Germany	4,964,523	245,334	5,209,857
Hungary	180,500	2,040	182,540
India	2,166,238	4660,456	2,632,694
Indonesia	352,172	112,644	464,816
Iran	1,359,520	35,901	1,395,421
Italy	661,100	182,139	843,239
Japan	6,862,161	1,072,355	7,934,516
Malaysia	447,002	42,267	489,269

Mexico	942,876	618,176	1,561,052
Netherlands	50,620	25,981	76,601
Poland	819,000	65,133	884,133
Portugal	101,680	24,335	126,015
Romania	279,320	17,178	296,498
Russia	595,839	126,592	722,431
Serbia	8,720	1,355	10,075
Slovakia	461,340	0	461,340
Slovenia	202,570	10,179	212,749
South Africa	222,981	150,942	373,923
South Korea	3,158,417	354,509	3,512,926
Spain	1,812,688	357,390	2,170,078
Sweden	128,738	27,600	156,338
Taiwan	183,986	42,370	226,356
Thailand	313,442	685,936	999,378
Turkey	510,931	358,674	869,605
Ukraine	65,646	3,649	69,295
United Kingdom	999,460	90,679	1,090,139
United States	2,246,470	3,462,382	5,708,852
Uzbekistan	110,200	7,700	117,900
Supplementary	302,450	110,109	412,559
TOTAL	**47,952,995**	**13,761,694**	**61,714,689**

Source: OICA

APPENDIX C
IMPORTANT BANKING LEGISLATION

The most important laws that have affected the banking industry in the United States are listed below.

(The Main Library of the FDIC, located at the FDIC offices in Washington, D.C., has legislative histories of these laws. These legislative histories help provide a better understanding of lawmakers' intent for the purpose and scope of the laws. The public can make an appointment to use these materials by contacting the FDIC Library.)

National Bank Act of 1934 (Chapter 106, 13 STAT. 99).
Established a national banking system and the chartering of national banks

Federal Reserve Act of 1913 (P.L. 63-43, 38 STAT. 251, 12 USC 221).
Established the Federal Reserve System as the central banking system of the U.S.

To Amend the National Banking Laws and the Federal Reserve Act (P.L. 69-639, 44 STAT. 1224)
Also known as the McFadden Act of 1927. Prohibited interstate banking.

Banking Act of 1933 (P.L. 73-66, 48 STAT. 162)
Also known as the Glass-Steagall Act. Established the FDIC as a temporary agency. Separated commercial banking from investment banking, establishing them as separate lines of commerce.

Banking Act of 1935 (P.L. 74-305, 49 STAT. 684)
Established the FDIC as a permanent agency of the government.

Federal Deposit Insurance Act of 1950 (P.L. 81-797, 64STAT. 873)
Revised and consolidated earlier FDIC legislation into one ACT. Embodied the basic authority for the operation of the FDIC.

Bank Holding Company Act of 1956 (P.L. 84-511, 701 STAT. 133)
Required Federal Reserve Board approval for the establishment of a bank

holding company. Prohibited bank holding companies headquartered in one state from acquiring a bank in another state.

International Banking Act of 1978 (P.L. 95-369, 92 STAT. 607)
Brought foreign banks within the federal regulatory framework. Required deposit insurance for branches of foreign banks engaged in retail deposit taking in the U.S.

Financial Institutions Regulatory and Interest Rate Control Act of 1978 (P.L. 95-630, 92 STAT. 3641)
Also known as FIRIRCA. Created the Federal Financial Institutions Examination Council. Established limits and reporting requirements for bank inside transactions. Created major statutory provisions regarding electronic fund transfers.

Depository Institutions Deregulation and Monetary Control Act of 1980 (P.L. 96-221, 94 STAT. 132)
Also known as DIDMCA. Established "NOW Accounts." Began the phase-out of interest rate ceilings on deposits. Established the Depository Institutions Deregulation Committee. Granted new powers to thrift institutions. Raised the deposit insurance ceiling to $100,000.

Depository Institutions Act of 1982 (P.L. 97-320, 96 STAT. 1469)
Also known as Garn-St. Germain. Expanded FDIC powers to assist troubled banks. Established the Net Worth Certificate program. Expanded the powers of thrift institutions.

Competitive Equality Banking Act of 1987 (P.L. 100-86, 101 STAT. 552)
Also known as CEBA. Established new standards for expedited funds availability. Recapitalized the Federal Savings & Loan Insurance Company (FSLIC). Expanded FDIC authority for open bank assistance transactions, including bridge banks.

Financial Institutions Reform, Recovery and Enforcement Act of 1989 (P.L. 101-73, 103 STAT. 183)
Also known as FIRREA. FIRREA's purpose was to restore the public's

confidence in the savings and loan industry. FIRREA abolished the Federal Savings & Loan Insurance Corporation (FSLIC), and the FDIC was given the responsibility of insuring the deposits of thrift institutions in its place.

The FDIC insurance fund created to cover thrifts was named the Savings Association Insurance Fund (SAIF), while the fund covering banks was called the Bank Insurance Fund (BIF).

FIRREA also abolished the Federal Home Loan Bank Board. Two new agencies, the Federal Housing Finance Board (FHFB) and the Office of Thrift Supervision (OTS), were created to replace it.

Finally, FIRREA created the Resolution Trust Corporation (RTC) as a temporary agency of the government. The RTC was given the responsibility of managing and disposing of the assets of the failed institutions. An Oversight Board was created to provide supervisory authority over the policies of the RTC, and the Resolution Funding Corporation (RFC) was created to provide funding for RTC operations.

Crime Control Act of 1990 (P.L. 101-647, 104 STAT. 4789)
Title XXV of the Crime Control Act, known as the Comprehensive Thrift and Bank Fraud Prosecution and Taxpayer Recovery Act of 1990, greatly expanded the authority of federal regulators to combat financial fraud.

This act prohibited undercapitalized banks from making golden parachute and other indemnification payments to institution-affiliated parties. It also increased penalties and prison time for those convicted of bank crimes, increased the powers and authority of the FDIC to take enforcement actions against institutions operating in an unsafe or unsound manner, and gave regulators new procedural powers to recover assets improperly diverted from financial institutions.

Federal Deposit Insurance Corporation Improvement Act of 1991
(P.L. 102-242, 105 STAT. 2236)
Also known as FDICIA. FDICIA greatly increased the powers and authority of the FDIC. Major provisions recapitalized the Bank Insurance Fund and allowed the FDIC to strengthen the fund by borrowing from the Treasury. The act mandated a least-cost resolution method and prompt resolution approach to problem and failing banks and ordered the creations of a risk-based insurance assessment scheme. Brokered deposits and the

solicitation of deposits were restricted, as were the non-bank activities of insured state banks. FDICIA created new supervisory and regulatory examination standards and put forth new capital requirements for banks. It also expanded prohibitions against insider activities and created new Truth in Savings provisions.

Housing and Community Development Act of 1992 (P.L. 102-550, 106 STAT. 3672)
Established regulatory structure for government-sponsored enterprises (GSEs), combated money laundering , and provided regulatory relief to financial institutions.

RTC Completion Act (P.L. 103-204, 107 STAT. 2369)
Required the RTC to adopt a series of management reforms and to implement provisions designed to improve the agency's record in providing business opportunities to minorities and women when issuing RTC contracts or selling assets. Expanded the existing affordable housing programs of the RTC and the FDIC by broadening the potential affordable housing stock of the two agencies. Increased the statute of limitations on RTC civil lawsuits from three years to five, or to the period provided in state law, whichever is longer. In cases in which the statute of limitations has expired, claims can be revived for fraud and intentional misconduct resulting in unjust enrichment or substantial loss to the thrift. Provided final funding for the RTC and established a transition plan for transfer of RTC resources to the FDIC. The RTC's sunset date was set at Dec. 31, 1995, at which time the FDIC will assumed its conservatorship and receivership functions.

Riegle Community Development and Regulatory Improvement Act of 1994 (P.L. 103-325, 108 STAT. 2160)
Established a Community Development Financial Institutions Fund, a wholly owned government corporation that would provide financial and technical assistance to CDFIs.

Contained several provisions aimed at curbing the practice of "reverse redlining" in which non-bank lenders target low and moderate income homeowners, minorities and the elderly for home equity loans on abusive terms. Relaxed capital requirements and other regulations to encourage the private sector secondary market for small business loans.

Contained more than 50 provisions to reduce bank regulatory burden and paperwork requirements. Required the Treasury Dept. to develop ways to substantially reduce the number of currency transactions filed by financial institutions. Contained provision aimed at shoring up the National Flood Insurance Program.

Riegle-Neal Interstate Banking and Branching Efficiency Act of 1994 (P.L. 103-328, 108 STAT. 2338)

Permitted adequately capitalized and managed bank holding companies to acquire banks in any state one year after enactment. Concentration limits apply and CRA evaluations by the Federal Reserve are required before acquisitions are approved. Beginning June 1, 1997, allowed interstate mergers between adequately capitalized and managed banks, subject to concentration limits, state laws and CRA evaluations. Extended the statute of limitations to permit the FDIC and RTC to revive lawsuits that had expired under state statutes of limitations.

Economic Growth and Regulatory paperwork Reduction Act of 1996 (P.L. 104-208, 110 STAT. 3009)

Modified financial institution regulations, including regulations impeding the flow of credit from the lending institutions to businesses and consumers. Amended the Truth in Lending Act and the Real Estate Settlement Procedures Act of 1974 to streamline the mortgage lending process.

Amended the FDIA to eliminate or revise various application, notice, and recordkeeping requirements to reduce regulatory burden and the cost of credit. Amended the Fair Credit Reporting Act to strengthen consumer protections relating to credit reporting agency practices.

Established consumer protections for potential clients of consumer repair services. Clarified lender liability and federal agency liability issues under the CERCLA. Directed FDIC to impose a special assessment on depository institutions to recapitalize the SAIF, aligned SAIF assessment rates.

Gramm-Leach-Bliley Act of 1999 (P.L. 106-102, 113 STAT. 1338)

Repealed last vestiges of the Glass-Steagall Act of 1933. Modified portions of the Bank Holding Company Act to allow affiliations between banks and insurance underwriters. While preserving authority of states to regulate insurance, the act prohibited state actions that have the effect of preventing bank affiliated firms from selling insurance on an equal basis with other insurance agents. Created a new financial holding company under section 4 of the BHCA, authorized to engage in: underwriting and selling insurance and securities, conducting both commercial and merchant banking, investing in and developing real estate and other "complementary" activities." There are limits on the kinds of non-financial activities these new entities may engage in.

Allowed national banks to underwrite municipal bonds. Restricted the disclosure of nonpublic customer information by financial institutions. All financial institutions must provide customers the opportunity to "opt out" of the sharing of the customers' nonpublic information with unaffiliated third parties. The Act imposed criminal penalties on anyone who obtains customer information from a financial institution under false pretenses.

Amended the Community Reinvestment Act to require that financial holding companies cannot be formed before their insured depository institutions receive and maintain a satisfactory CRA rating. Also required public disclosure of bank-community CRA-related agreements. Granted some regulatory relief to small institutions in the shape of reducing the frequency of the CRA examinations if they have received outstanding or satisfactory ratings. Prohibited affiliations and acquisitions between commercial firms and unitary thrift institutions.

Made significant changes in the operation of the Federal Home Loan bank System, easing membership requirements and loosening restriction on the use of FHLB funds.

International Money Laundering Abatement and Financial Anti-Terrorism Act of 2001* (P.L. 107-56)

Legislation designed to prevent terrorists and others from using the U.S. financial system anonymously to move funds obtained from or destined for illegal activity. It authorized and required additional record keeping and reporting by financial institutions and greater scrutiny of accounts held for foreign banks and of private banking conducted for foreign persons.

The law required financial institutions to establish anti-money laundering programs and imposed various standards on money-transmitting businesses. It amended criminal anti-money laundering statutes and procedures for forfeitures in money laundering cases and required further cooperation between financial institutions and government agencies in fighting money laundering.

Sarbanes-Oxley Act of 2002* (P.L. 107-204)

Sarbanes-Oxley established the Public Company Oversight Board to regulate public accounting firms that audit publicly-traded companies. It prohibited such firms from providing other services to such companies along with the audit. It required that CEOs and CFOs certify the annual and quarterly reports of publicly traded companies.

The Act authorized, and in some cases required, that the securities and Exchange Commission (SEC) issues the rules governing audits. The law required that insiders may no longer trade their company's securities during pension fund blackout periods. It mandated various studies including a study of the involvement of investment banks and financial advisors in the scandals preceding the legislation. Also included were whistle blower protections, and new federal criminal laws, including a ban on alteration of documents.

Fair and Accurate Credit Transaction Act of 2003* (P.L. 108-159)

The Fair and Accurate Credit Transactions (FACT) Act contained extensive amendments to the Fair Credit Reporting Act and was designed to improve the accuracy and transparency of the national credit reporting system and preventing identity theft and assisting victims. It contained provisions enhancing consumer rights in situations involving alleged identity theft, credit scoring, and claims of inaccurate information. It required use of consumer reports to provide certain information to consumers who are offered credit on terms that are materially less favorable than the offers that the creditor makes to a substantial portion of its consumers. Companies that share consumer information among affiliated companies, must provide consumers notice and an opt-out for sharing of such information if the information will be used for marketing purposes.

Descriptions taken from "Major Statutes Affecting Financial Institutions and Markets," Congressional Research Service

Source: FDIC

APPENDIX D
Fortune 500: Ranking of America's largest corporations for 2010
(1-100)

RANK	COMPANY	REVENUES ($ MILLIONS)	PROFITS ($ MILLIONS)
1	Wal-Mart (sic) Stores	408,214.0	14,335.0
2	Exxon Mobil	284,650.0	19,280.0
3	Chevron	163,527.0	10,483.0
4	General Electric	156,779.0	11,025.0
5	Bank of America Corp.	150,450.0	6,276.0
6	ConocoPhillips	139,515.0	4,858
7	AT&T	123,018.0	12,535.0
8	Ford Motor	118,308.0	2,717.0
9	J.P. Morgan Chase & Co.	115,632.0	11,728.0
10	Hewlett-Packard	114,552.0	7,660.0
11	Berkshire Hathaway	112,493.0	8,055.0
12	Citigroup	108,785.0	-1,606.0
13	Verizon Communications	107,808.0	3,651.0
14	McKesson	106,632.0	823.0
15	General Motors	104,589.0	N.A.
16	American International Group	103,189.0	-10,949.0

17	Cardinal Health	99,612.9	1,151.6
18	CVS Caremark	98,729.0	3,696.0
19	Wells Fargo	98,636.0	12,275.0
20	International Business Machines	95,758.0	13,425.0
21	United Health Group	87,138.0	3,822.0
22	Proctor & Gamble	79,697.0	13,436.0
23	Kroger	76,733.2	70.0
24	AmerisourceBergen	71,789.0	503.4
25	Costco Wholesale	71,422.0	1,086.0
26	Valero Energy	70,035.0	-1,982.0
27	Archer Daniels Midland	69,207.0	1,707.0
28	Boeing	68,281.0	1,312.0
29	Home Depot	66,176.0	2,661.0
30	Target	65,357.0	2,488.0
31	Wellpoint	65,028.1	4,745.9
32	Walgreen	63,335.0	2,006.0
33	Johnson & Johnson	61,897.0	12,266.0
34	State Farm Insurance Cos.	61,479.6	766.7
35	Medco Health Solutions	59,804.2	1,280.3
36	Microsoft	58,437.0	14,569.0
37	United Technologies	52,920.0	3,829.0
38	Dell	52,902.0	1,433.0

39	Goldman Sachs Group	51,673.0	13,385.0
40	Pfizer	50,009.0	8,635.0
41	Marathon Oil	49,403.0	1,463.0
42	Lowe's	47,220.0	1,783.0
43	United Parcel Service	45,297.0	2,152.0
44	Lockheed Martin	45,189.0	3,024.0
45	Best Buy	45,015.0	1,003.0
46	Dow Chemical	44,945.0	648.0
47	Supervalu	44,564.0	-2,855.0
48	Sears Holdings	44,043.0	235.0
49	International Assets Holding	43,604.4	27.6
50	PepsiCo	43,232.0	5,946.0
51	MetLife	41,098.0	-2,246.0
52	Safeway	40,850.7	-1,097.5
53	Kraft Foods	40,386.0	3,021.0
54	Freddie Mac	37,614.0	-21,553.0
55	Sysco	36,853.3	1,055.9
56	Apple	36,537.0	5,704.0
57	Walt Disney	36,149.0	3,307.0
58	Cisco Systems	36,117.0	6,134.0
59	Comcast	35,756.0	3,638.0
60	FedEx	35,497.0	98.0
61	Northrop Grumman	35,291.0	1,686.0

62	Intel	35,127.0	4,369.0
63	Aetna	34,764.1	1,276.5
64	New York Life Insurance	34,014.3	682.7
65	Prudential Financial	32,688.0	3,124.0
66	Caterpillar	32,396.0	895.0
67	Sprint Nextel	32,260.0	-2,436.0
68	Allstate	32,013.0	854.0
69	General Dynamics	31,981.0	2,394.0
70	Morgan Stanley	31,515.	1,346.0
71	Liberty Mutual Insurance Group	31,094.0	1,023.0
72	Coca-Cola	30,990.0	6,824.0
73	Humana	30,960.4	1,039.7
74	Honeywell International	30,908.0	2,153.0
75	Abbott Laboratories	30,764.7	5,745.8
76	News Corp.	30,423.0	-3,378.0
77	HCA	30,052.0	1,054.0
78	Sunoco	29,630.0	-329.0
79	Hess	29,569.0	740.0
80	Ingram Micro	29,515.4	202.1
81	Fannie Mae	29,065.0	-71,969.0
82	Time Warner	28,842.0	2,468.0
83	Johnson Controls	28,497.0	-338.0

84	Delta Air Lines	28,063.0	-1,237.0
85	Merck	27,428.3	12,901.3
86	DuPont	27,328.0	1,755.0
87	Tyson Foods	27,165.0	-537.0
88	American Express	26,730.0	2,130.0
89	Rite Aid	26,289.5	-2,915.4
90	TIAA-CREF	26,278.0	-459.1
91	CHS	25,729.9	381.4
92	Enterprise GP Holdings	25,510.9	204.1
93	Massachusetts Mutual Life Insurance	25,423.6	-115.1
94	Phillip Morris International	25,035.0	6,342.0
95	Raytheon	24,881.0	1,935.0
96	Express Scripts	24,748.9	827.6
97	Hartford Financial Services	24,701.0	-887.0
98	Travelers Cos.	24,680.0	3,622.0
99	Publix Supermarkets	24,515.0	1,161.4
100	Amazon.com	24,509.0	902.0

Source: Fortune

APPENDIX E
Key Facts Regarding Pharmaceutical Research and Development[2]

Research and Development (R&D)

- Time to develop a drug = 10 to 15 years[1]

Development Costs

- Cost to develop a drug
  2005 = $1.3 billion[2]
  2001 = $802 million[3]
  1987 = $318 million[3]
  1975 = $138 million[3]

- Cost to develop a biologic
  2005 = $1.2 billion[4]

R&D Spending

Year	PhRMA members[5]	Total industry[6]
2009	$45.8 billion (est.)	$65.3 billion (est.)
2008	$47.4 billion	$63.7 billion
2007	$47.9 billion	$63.2 billion
2006	$43.4 billion	$56.1 billion
2005	$39.9 billion	$51.8 billion
2004	$37.0 billion	$47.6 billion
2000	$26.0 billion	not available
1990	$8.4 billion	not available
1980	$2.0 billion	not available

Percentage of Sales That Went to R&D in 2009[7]

Domestic R&D
As a percentage of domestic sales = 19.0%

Total R&D
As a percentage of total sales = 16.0%

Economic Impact of the Biopharmaceutical Sector[8]

Direct jobs =
686,422 in 2006 (most recent data)

Total jobs (including indirect and induced jobs) =
3.2 million in 2006 (most recent data)

Approvals

- Drugs and biologics approved in 2009 = 34[9]
- In the 27 years since the Orphan Drug Act was established, nearly 350 orphan drugs have been approved.[10]
- Only 2 of 10 marketed drugs return revenues that match or exceed R&D costs.[11]

Medicines in Development

2010 = 2,950 compounds[12]
1999 = 1,800 compounds[13]

Value of Medicines

- **Cancer:** Since 1980, life expectancy for cancer patients has increased about **3 years,** and 83% of those gains are attributable to new treatments, including medicines.[14] Another study found that medicines specifically account for 50% to 60% of increases in survival rates since 1975.[15]
- **Cardiovascular Disease:** According to the American Heart Association (AHA), death rates for cardiovascular disease fell a dramatic **26.4%** between 1999 and 2005.[16] The AHA lists better control of high blood pressure and high cholesterol, and reduced tobacco use, as factors in the improvement.[17]
- **HIV/AIDS:** Since new medicines were approved in 1995, the AIDS death rate has dropped **more than 70%.**[18] Between 2006 and 2007 the death rate fell 10% – the largest single-year decline since 1998.[19]

Sales

- Generic share of market[20]
  2000 = 49%
  2009 = 74%

Acknowledgments

First, I would like to express my deepest gratitude to my bride and friend of 55 years Rose Marie (Teddi) who provided editing help and knowledge from the very beginning, with criticism engulfed with love.

My very bright granddaughter, Clare Robinson, while still in high school, was supportive in typing duties and suggesting changes. Clare is now a freshman at Notre Dame University in South Bend, Indiana.

My daughter Rachel Pustulka, on weekend visits away from her home in Lorain Ohio, was a source of brilliant word substitution and support.

Susan Tabar is a writer with an impressive literary and news background, including work for CNN and Dr. Henry Kissinger. She provided both good editing and balance.

Keith Gave, a former newspaper writer for the Detroit Free Press and the Dallas Morning News and currently a faculty journalism advisor and instructor at Washtenaw Community College provided detailed editing, clarity and punch where needed.

Paula Bradley, an editor with a pure sense of grammar and structure, transformed my oratorical form of writing into a visual read. Paula worked with me for six months after I had completed my first manuscript, and refined it into a readable document. She is great and I commend her to the next writer.

This work was a labor of nearly five years. I was inspired to start my research by the sound bites of knowledge from newspapers and magazines, particularly *The Week*. In the beginning, the libraries of St. Clair County, Michigan, Manatee County, Florida and the Jane Bancroft Cook Library at the New College of Florida provided critical research assistance.

Edward J. Robinson149